Gateway Arch and Indiana Dunes National Parks Planning Guide

Kenneth Perry

Have a great adventure!
Kenneth Perry

Kenneth Perry

Copyright © 2021 ALL RIGHTS RESERVED.

Written by Kenneth Perry
Reviewed by Cindy Perry
Edited by Tiffany N. O'Brien
Photographs by Kenneth Perry unless credited otherwise.

No part of this book may be reproduced or transmitted in any form by any means, electronic or mechanical, including photocopying and recording, or by any information storage and retrieval system, except as may be expressly permitted in writing from NationalParkPlanningGuidesInfo@gmail.com.

ISBN-10: - 1-946490-39-3
ISBN-13: - 978-1-946490-39-1

DEDICATION

I would like to dedicate this collection of planning guides to two important people in my life: my son, Joe Perry, for revitalizing me with a desire to search out and enjoy this beautiful country and its natural resources and explore all of the National Parks; and my lovely wife, Cindy Perry, who has supported me in the writing of this planning guide. I am very fortunate to find a special woman that not only enjoys nature, travel, etc., but is always up for the next adventure that I come up with.

CONTENTS

	Copyritght	i
	Dedication	ii
1	How to use the planning guide	1
2	Gateway Arch Overview	3
	ADA Accessibility	4
	Park Visitation	8
	Historical Temperature and Rainfall	9
3	Gateway Arch History	10
4	Gateway Arch Activities	12
5	Gateway Arch Personal Favorites	15
6	Gateway Arch Transportation	20
	St. Louis, MO Amtrak (STL) and Car rental	20
	St. Louis Lambert International Airport (XWA)	20
	MidAmerica St. Louis Airport (BLV)	22
7	Other Park Sites Near Gateway Arch	23
8	Indiana Dunes Overview	43
	ADA Accessibility	43
	Park Visitation	46
	Historical Temperature and Rainfall	47
9	Indiana Dunes History	48
10	Indiana Dunes Activities	49
	National Park Scheduled Events	49
	Backcountry Camping	58
	Beach-going and Swimming	58
	Bicycles	60

	Bird Watching Festival	61
	Boating	61
	Cross country skiing/ Snowshoeing	61
	Fishing	62
	Geocaching	62
	Hiking Trails	63
	Historical Sites	68
	Houses of the Future	69
	Horseback Riding	71
	Indiana Dunes State Park	72
	Things to do outside the park	73
11	Indiana Dunes Personal Favorites	75
	Bailly Homestead	75
	BARK Ranger Program	76
	Beaches	77
	Biking	77
	Chellberg Farm	78
	Hiking	80
	Sand Dunes	82
	Houses of the Future	83
12	Indiana Dunes Accommodations	89
	Camping in the park	89
	Camping near Indiana Dunes National Park	90
	Hotels near Indiana Dunes	91
13	Indiana Dunes Restaurants	95
	Porter, Indiana	95

	Chesterton, Indiana	96
	Portage, Indiana	98
	Michigan City, Indiana	100
14	Indiana Dunes Transportation	107
	Chicago, IL Amtrak	107
	Chicago, IL, O'Hare International Airport (ORD)	107
	Chicago, IL, Midway International Airport (MDW)	112
15	Park Units near Indiana Dunes	113
16	National Park Planning Guides	120
17	About the Author	122

1 HOW TO USE THE PLANNING GUIDE

The National Park Planning Guide is a collection of the most current information to help plan a "great adventure". The book is designed to eliminate hours of research for all the things you need to consider when planning your vacation. Instead it puts all of the information in an organized and easy-to-use format to help you plan your vacation.

This book will provide:

- Overview - Basic park information and unique park specific items like Park Shuttles
- ADA Accessibility - Within the park.
- History - Briefly talk about people, culture, geology etc.
- Accommodations - Detailed Lodging and Campgrounds inside and outside the park
- Booking Tips - When to book accommodations, tours, etc.
- Activities - Inside and outside of the park
- Restaurants - Inside and outside of the park, listed by type of food
- Other Government Parks in the area
- Also included National and State Parks Units - Fort Union Trading Post National Historic Site, Knife River National Historic Site, Ft Buford State Historic Site, and Missouri-Yellowstone Confluence Interpretive Center

This planning guide is available in both eBook (downloadable to your iPhone, Android, iPad, tablet, or laptop) and paperback.

Make sure that you visit our website: NationalParkPlanningGuides.com for additional high level planning information and more, such as:

- Blog with RSS feed - All of the latest information on the planning guides
- Photos - Please feel free to copy and use any of the photos that are on the website
- Online Store - find your books easily on Amazon with direct links to purchase the books
- Revisions - Updated information
- Planning Information - Includes historical temperature/rainfall/accommodations/comprehensive activities matrix for all National Parks
- Book Releases - Includes both current and books planned to be

released within the year
- Comments - Leave a comment and/or register for notifications of book updates and releases

Even though I am focusing my eBooks and paperback books on the 62 National Parks, there is so much more that the National Park Service provides for us to visit and explore. These include:

National Battlefields (11)	National Battlefields Parks (4)
National Battlefields Site (1)	National Military Parks (9)
National Historic Parks (58)	National Historic Sites (76)
International Historic Sites (1)	National Lakeshores (3)
National Memorials (31)	National Monuments (85)
National Parks (62)	National Parkways (4)
National Preserves (19)	National Reserves (2)
National Recreation Areas (18)	National Rivers (5)
National Wild and Scenic Rivers and Riverways (10)	National Scenic Trails (3)
National Seashores (10)	Other Designations (11)

Total of 423 National Park Service units as of January 11, 2021

Thank you and have a great adventure…

2 GATEWAY ARCH OVERVIEW

Source: NPS

This park was first designated as the Jefferson Expansion National Memorial in 1935 and became Gateway Arch National Park in 2018. The park covers approximately 90 acres and is located in St. Louis, MO. It was visited by 2,055,309 people in 2019. I used the 2019 visitation numbers since there were more representative than those found during the COVID-19 pandemic of 2020.

Contact Information: 11 North 4th Street St. Louis, MO 63102

Website: https://www.nps.gov/jeff/index.htm

Physical Address: 11 North 4th Street St. Louis, MO 63102

Phone number: (314) 655-1600

GPS Coordinates:
Gateway Arch: N 38°37'29" W 90°11'06"

Costs:
Entrance Fee is $3.00 per person. Entry is free for ages 16 and younger and pass holders.

If you have a 4th grader in your family, a special FREE pass is available for the entire family. Go to this website for information: www.everykidinapark.gov

ADA Accessibility: The National Park Service and its partners welcome all visitors and make many efforts to accommodate people with disabilities in the Old Courthouse, the Gateway Arch complex, and on the park grounds. The park has accessible exhibits and programs and offers various assistive devices. The museum exhibits and media in the six galleries at the Gateway Arch will have multiple accessibility features for physical and programmatic accessibility including: tactile exhibits, audio descriptions, and computer simulations that are visitor directed through a touchpad.

"We do not offer access for wheelchairs, scooters, or strollers to the top levels of the Gateway Arch or the Old Courthouse." Source: NPS

The top of the Gateway Arch is not wheelchair accessible. To reach it and return, you must manage a minimum of 96 steps, which are separated by 6 flights of stairs. Please be aware you may need to stand for 30 to 60 minutes or longer, especially during the busy summer season. There are no seats or restrooms at the top of the Arch. In the new museum there is a representation of the keystone piece of the Gateway Arch which will replicate the experience as much as possible for visitors who cannot make the trip to the top. In consultation with our universal design citizen group, a keystone hub was designed to house a live feed to replicate the view to the west and east from the top of the observation deck of the Gateway Arch.

Visitors on the autism spectrum and their companions will find useful information in this social story about coming to the visitor center and riding to the top of the Arch.

Please call ahead to confirm availability for assistive listening devices and request devices at the Information Desk in the lobby.

Old Courthouse

There is a wheelchair lift on the Broadway entrance of the building (west side). Until the permanent ramp opens, a portable ramp will remain outside of the Dred Scott exhibit gallery doors to provide access to the Old Courthouse via the lift.

Most of the first floor of the Old Courthouse is accessible to wheelchairs, but the upper floors of the Old Courthouse are reachable only by climbing stairs.

Steps above the first floor:

Between first and second floor   33 steps
Between second and third floor   22 steps
Between third floor and balcony 22 steps

The floor level changes in the upper floors, and single steps separate these different levels.

Access Pass

If you are a U.S. citizen and have a permanent disability, you may obtain a free Access Pass at the Gateway Arch Information Desk or at the Old Courthouse Museum Shop. The passport allows free admission to federal areas which charge an entrance fee and provides reductions for other types of user fees.

Service Dogs

Service dogs are welcome at the park.

There are around 65 steps in the Grand Staircase between the Arch

Grounds and Lenore K. Sullivan Boulevard, which borders the levee. There are two ramps providing access from Lenore K. Sullivan Boulevard to the Gateway Arch grounds. There are no designated accessible parking spaces on the levee.

For further information, please contact NPS through their information line at 314-655-1700 or e-mail them through the website at: www.nps.gov/jeff. Missouri relay at (voice) 1-800-735-2966 provides services for those who are hearing impaired.

Source: NPS

Passport Stamp Locations: https://www.eparks.com/documents/cancellations.pdf

St. Louis; Kansas City Mule; Ann Rutledge; Texas Eagle; Trails and Rails Lincoln Service; Trails and Rails Missouri River Runner; Old Courthouse

Visitor Centers

- **Main Visitor Center** - Information, park movie $$, park passes, exhibits, museum, and gift store

- **Campgrounds in the park**
- None

- **Hotels and Lodges in the park**
- None

- **Ranger Led Program**
- https://www.nps.gov/jeff/planyourvisit/calendar.htm
- Only 1 program for August 2019; none for September 2019

This is the newest National Park designated by the United States Congress which was previously a memorial.

The quote below is from the Gateway Arch National Park website:

"The park is a memorial to Thomas Jefferson's role in opening the West, to the pioneers who helped shape its history, and to Dred Scott who sued for his freedom in the Old Courthouse."
Source: NPS

Parking

Parking in the downtown area of St. Louis can be problematic for cars and near impossible for visitors traveling in RVs, Trailers, or while towing.

There are a few options for those in automobiles. I found getting into the city early and visiting on Saturday and Sunday offers the best chance of getting a parking spot. Another option is use public transportation to get to the Gateway Arch.

Several parking garages, in walking distance to the Gateway Arch, offer parking for automobiles only. Parking Information website: https://www.bestparking.com/st-louis-parking/neighborhoods/gateway-arch-parking/?daily=1

If you have an RV and are towing a vehicle, my recommendation for your visit, approximately six miles past the arch to the west on I-64 take the exit to South Brentwood Boulevard and head south. You will find big parking areas at Home Depot, Menards, and Walmart stores with easy return access to I-64.

When do most visitors visit Gateway Arch National Park?

This will give you a good overview of the attendance based on monthly totals times 1,000 for 2019.

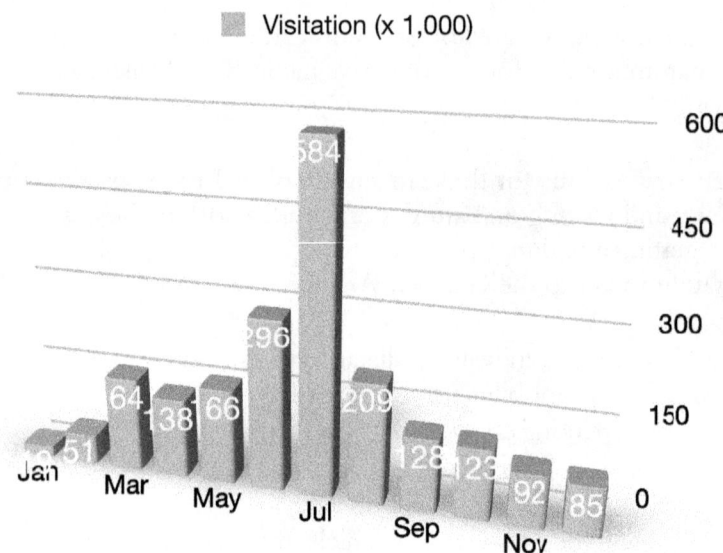

Source: <u>NationalParkPlanningGuides.com</u>

Average Temperature: (high/low)

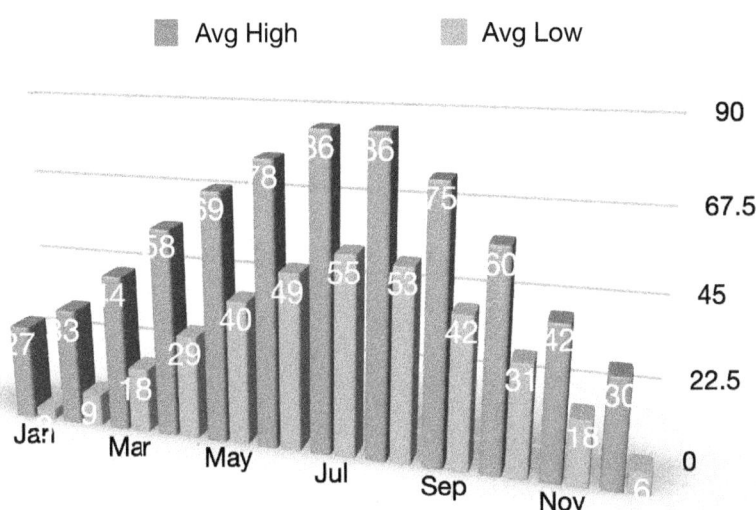

Average Precipitation:

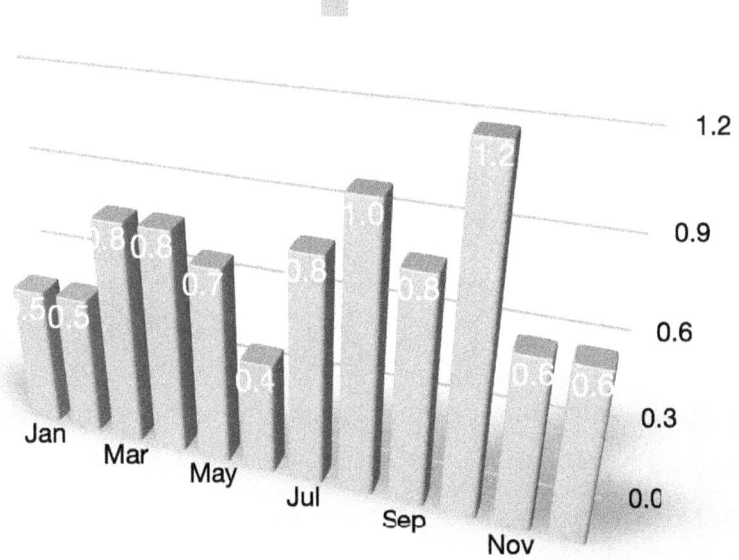

3 GATEWAY ARCH HISTORY

Arch History

In 1933, Luther Ely Smith envisioned a memorial to stimulate the economy in the riverfront district. In 1935, the building of the memorial was passed by congress and signed by President Franklin Delano Roosevelt.
A competition of 172 designs was won by Eero Saarinen in 1948. Construction of the arch did not commence until 1961 with the pouring of the foundations, and in 1963 the first steel was laid. The arch was completed in 1965.

Opening up the west

Opening of the west started with a vision from Thomas Jefferson to expand the growing population west of the Mississippi. To do that, the Louisiana Purchase and the explorations of Lewis and Clark took place. This opened up fur trading posts west of the Mississippi and later came the rapid expansion of families homesteading and the Gold Rush.

President Thomas Jefferson

Thomas Jefferson served as the 3rd President of the United States from 1801 t0 1809. He strengthened and promoted trade and doubled the size of the United States with the Louisiana Purchase.

Louisiana Purchase

In 1803 the purchase of the Louisiana Territory from France added 828,000 square miles, 530,000,000 acres for 15 million dollars (approximately $0.03/acre). In addition to the western expansion, another benefit was to gain control of the shipping lane from New Orleans up the Mississippi River and other river systems.

Lewis & Clark Corp of Discovery

Meriwether Lewis was President Thomas Jefferson's personal secretary and was handpicked to lead the expedition. After extensive training and preparation, Meriwether Lewis and William Clark led an expedition up the Missouri River in hopes of finding a Northwest Passage to the Pacific Ocean for the purpose of opening trade routes to the Orient.

Fur Trading

From the early 1800s trappers and mountain men, mostly in small quantities, traded with tribes west of the Mississippi. Before that time, tribes traded with Hudson's Bay Company forts in Canada. Hudson's Bay Company was run by the British Government. President Jefferson sent General Atkinson to negotiate treaties of "friendship and trade" with the tribes to only trade with United States Companies. In the early 1800s, privately owned fur trading companies appeared all along the rivers which ran west of the Mississippi.

Westward Expansion

Homesteading began in 1862 in an effort to entice people to settle the west. To do this, the government offered 160 acres of land to anyone that moved and established a new home and lived there for five continuous years.

Civil Rights

In 1857, Dred Scott vs. Sanford, an African American slave, sued for the freedom of himself, his wife, and their two children. The Supreme Court in a 7 to 2 decision stated that black people were not included in the meaning of the word Citizen in the Constitution. It wasn't until after the Civil War and the thirteenth amendment was written that the Supreme Court reversed its decision.

4 ACTIVITIES

National Park Scheduled Events

National Park Scheduled Events
Other than the Junior Ranger Program, there are few activities listed on the park's calendar. Be sure to check the park calendar and Facebook for the latest and up-to-date activities. The summer of 2019 was pretty light when we were there.

Gateway Arch Attractions:

Museum

FREE - The museum is free and definitely worth visiting and spending some time in. The galleries include: Colonial St. Louis Gallery, Jefferson's Vision, New Frontiers, The Riverfront Era, Manifest Destiny, and Building the Dream.

Orientation Film

Website: https://www.gatewayarch.com/experience/

Phone: 877 982-1410

At most parks the orientation films are free. This is the first one that I have ever paid for, and we are glad we did. The film was very informative and did a great job sharing the history and showing how the structure was designed and constructed.

Tram ride inside the arch

Website: https://www.gatewayarch.com/experience/

Phone: 877 982-1410

Ascend to the top of the tallest monument in the United States in a tram car. The structure is 630 feet tall, 63 stories high, and weighs 43,000 tons.

Riverboat Cruise

Website: https://www.gatewayarch.com/experience/

Phone: 877 982-1410

The two replica paddle-wheel boats, Becky Tatcher and Tom Sawyer, offer daytime and nighttime views of the Arch and skyline of St. Louis. Some tours are ranger-led.

The St. Louis Riverfront Cruise - 1 hour cruise narrated by the captain or a National Park Service (NPS) Ranger.

Skyline Dinner Cruise - 2 hour evening cruise with great views of the night skyline. It features a dinner buffet and Dixieland band for entertainment.

Helicopter Rides

Website: https://www.gatewayhelicoptertours.com

Phone: 314 496-4494

Reservations are available for weekdays only. Weekends are walk-ins only.

Operation: April-November, 11am to 5pm (weather permitting)

Call for additional information.

Helicopter rides operate off of a barge located on the Mississippi River at the base of The Grand Staircase to the Gateway Arch. During our visit to the arch, the helicopter provided many rides in the area.

Church

I heard a humorous story from one of the city information workers inside the arch. She said that, "originally the Park Service wanted the church to be removed. The State/City government official said that would be impossible because that is where we were married and my wife would never let that happen", so it is still there.

5 PERSONAL FAVORITES

During your visit to the Gateway Arch, I would plan on trying to spend your day seeing all of the attractions at the arch. There are three paid attractions at Gateway Arch National Park that you don't want to miss. The tickets are available online, by phone, or at the Gateway Arch Visitor Center. I would highly recommend that you purchase your tickets a day in advance. We tried to book a tram ride at 1:30 pm, and there were only two time slots available for the day, so book early!

Museum - ★★★★★

FREE - The museum is free and definitely worth visiting and spending some time in.

Orientation Film - ★★★★★

The movie is a must see. It is very well done, and once you see the film you will have a deeper appreciation for the work that went into the job. Without the film showing the history and construction this would be like visiting just another building. I would recommend making the film your first stop.

Tram ride inside the arch - ★★★★★

This is one of those attractions that you will want to get your tickets ahead of time, as they book up quickly during the day. While your car climbs to the height of the observation deck you will be able to see construction through the observation window in each of the cars. Once at the observation area you will exit the tram car and have a great view to the east of Illinois and to the west of St. Louis, Missouri. Almost directly below is Busch Stadium, home of the St. Louis Cardinals. While we were at the top, there was a game going on and we could even see fireworks exploding over the park beneath us.

When you are at the base of the arch, look up to see the viewing portals at the top. The ride takes approximately four minutes going up but only three minutes to go down. You can spend as much time at the top as you would like. HINT: Each tram car holds five people and I got in last, which put me near the exit door with a window to check out the inside structure.

Riverboat Cruise - ★★★★★

As I was doing my research of all the activities, this was my first choice of things to do. I have been on the riverboats at Magic Kingdom in Disney World but wanted to experience it on the Mississippi River. I had been monitoring the water levels on the Mississippi and the week before we arrived the cruises opened. Within two days before we arrived, a big storm hit the Midwest and once again the Mississippi River went back into flood stage and the cruises ceased operation. We plan to return and take the day cruise in the afternoon and then the dinner cruise in the evening.

This is an attraction that you don't want to miss, however it will require some planning and a little luck, especially in the early season. Spring runoff can cause flooding on the Mississippi River which is just a thing that happens on the river and can be very unpredictable. April is a hit or miss for the operation of the cruise, but usually around the later part of May the schedule is pretty reliable. When in doubt, give them a call to check conditions.

There is Bus/RV Parking on a barge, if you are taking a riverboat cruise (typically closed during the early season or anytime that boat operations cease to operate due to high water and flooding).

Paved walking trails - ★★★★☆

It reminded me of being in Washington DC walking to different memorials on nice wide trails with the manicured lawns and abundance of trees in the park. They too have benches along the way where you can rest. The various network of paths allows you to arrive at the boat dock or helicopter ride without climbing the 65 steps at the base of the Gateway Arch.

Old Courthouse - ★★★★☆

There are many things to see at the Old Courthouse across from the arch. When you arrive at the courthouse the statue of Dred Scott and his wife on the front lawn. When entering the courtyard there is a gift shop on your left. Be sure to check out all of the various galleries found in the courthouse e.g., westward expansion, and the Dred Scott story.

When we were there a park ranger was in the center of the building where there is a high lofted ceiling. The ranger is usually there and talks about the unique acoustics. Then he positions you at a specific location and lets you experience an amazing phenomena.

Church - ★★★☆☆

The small church south of the arch is open but has limited scheduled times to view the inside.

6 GATEWAY ARCH TRANSPORTATION

St. Louis, MO Amtrak (STL) and Car rental

https://www.amtrak.com/stations/stl

Airports and Car Rental-
St. Louis, MO - St. Louis Lambert International Airport (XWA)
https://www.flystl.com

Company	Phone	Website
Air Canada	888 247-2262	https://www.aircanada.com
Air Choice One	866 435-9847	https://www.airchoiceone.com
Alaska Airlines	800 252-7522	https://www.alaskaair.com
American Airlines	800 433-7300	http://www.aa.com
Cape Air	800 227-3247	https://www.capeair.com/#/availability
Contour	888 332-6686	https://www.contourairlines.com/en
Delta	800 221-1212	delta.com
Frontier	800 401-9000	https://www.flyfrontier.com
Southwest	800 435-9792	https://www.southwest.com
Sun Country	651 905-2737	https://www.suncountry.com
United	800 864-8331	united.com

Company	Phone	Website
Volaris	855 865-2747	https://www.volaris.com

St Louis, MO Car Rental

Company	Phone	Website
Alamo	877 222-9075	
Avis	800 331-1212	http://www.avis.com
Budget	800 527-0700	
Enterprise Rent-A-Car	800 736-8222	
Hertz	800 654-3131	
National	800 227-7368	
Thrifty	800 847-4389	

Mascoutah, IL, MidAmerica St. Louis Airport (BLV)

http://www.flymidamerica.com/Pages/default.aspx

Company	Phone	Website
Allegiant	702 505-8888	https://www.allegiantair.com

Chicago, IL Car Rental

Company	Phone	Website
Enterprise Rent-A-Car	701 258-2636	http://www.enterprise.com

7 OTHER PARK SITES NEAR GATEWAY ARCH

Have you ever been on a vacation to visit a national park, and drive by one of the National Park units? Maybe you did not stop because you didn't know anything about the park unit, or didn't have the time to stop? I have included important information for each of those units in Kansas, Missouri, and Nebraska that will provide an overview of each of these sites.

Park Unit	City/State	Gateway Arch NP Driving Time	Distance
Brown b. Board of Education National Historic Site	Topeka, KS	4h 26m	311 miles
Fort Larned National Historic Site	Larned, KS	7h 33m	528 miles
Fort Scott National Historic Site	Fort Scott, KS	4h 42m	297 miles
Nicodemus National Historic Site	Nicodemus, KS	7h 55m	564 miles
Tallgrass Prairie National Preserve	Strong City, KS	5h 23m	379 miles
George Washington Carver National Monument	Diamond, MO	4h 1m	283 miles
Harry S Truman National Historic Site	Independence and Grandview, MO	3h 31m	242 miles
Ste. Genevieve National Historical Park	Ste. Genevieve, MO	59m	64 miles

		Gateway Arch NP	
Park Unit	City/State	Driving Time	Distance
Ulysses S Grant National Historic Site	St Louis, MO	19m	13 miles
Agate Fossil Beds National Monument	Harrison, NE	12h 58m	887
Homestead National Monument of America	Beatrice, NE	6h 28m	437
Scotts Bluff National Monument	Gering, NE	12h 9m	838
California National Historic Trail	CA, CO, ID, KS, MO, NE, NV, OR UT, WY	N/A	N/A
Lewis & Clark National Historic Trail	IA, ID, IL, IN, KS, KY, MO, MT, NE, ND, OH, OR, PA, SD, WA, WV	N/A	N/A
Missouri National Recreational River	Yankton, SD, NE	N/A	N/A
Mormon Pioneer National Historic Trail	IL, IA, NE, UT, WY	N/A	N/A
Niobrara National Scenic River	Valentine, NE	N/A	N/A
Oregon National Historic Trail	ID, KS, MO, NE, OR, WA, WY	N/A	N/A

Park Unit	City/State	Gateway Arch NP	
		Driving Time	Distance
Pony Express National Historic Trail	CA, CO, KS, MO, NE, NV, UT, WY	N/A	N/A
Santa Fe National Historic Trail	CO, KS, MO, NM, OK	N/A	N/A
Trail of Tears National Historic Trail	AL, AR, GA, IL, KY, MO, NC, OK, TN	N/A	N/A

Brown vs. Board of Education National Historic Site

Address: 1515 SE Monroe Street, Topeka, KS 66612

Phone: 785 354-4273

Website: https://www.nps.gov/brvb/index.htm

Overview: Congress established Brown vs. Board of Education National Historic Site in 1992. The Supreme Court's unanimous decision in 1954 in the case of Brown vs. Board of Education ruled that "segregated education was a denial of equal protection of the laws under the 14th Amendment". But segregated education did not stop in 1954. It took many years to integrate the schools of Topeka, KS and it was not without conflict. The park visitor center helped me to get a better picture of the inequalities, tribulations, and struggles the students dealt with to have equal opportunities for all races to attend public schools. The park visitor center is across the street from Monroe Elementary School (one of the four segregated schools).

The best time to visit this historic site is on the weekend, since you will be visiting multiple sites throughout the city of Topeka, KS and parking during the week would be difficult. In addition, the Visitor Center has a great audio tour you can download and play from your cell phone or tablet. App: National Park Service Tour by OnCell.

Fort Larned National Historic Site

Address: 1767 KS Hwy 156, Larned, KS 67550

Phone: 620 285-6911

Website: https://www.nps.gov/fols/index.htm

Overview: Congress established Fort Larned National Historic Site in 1964. Fort Larned provided escorts for transported mail, military supply wagons, and to keep peace on the plains from 1860 to 1878. The fort was one of many stopping points along the Santa Fe Trail. Not only were there soldiers at the fort, but Plains Indians, European Americans, Hispanic teamsters, homesteaders, hide hunters, scouts, and railroad workers were also present throughout its short history. Fort Larned housed Company A, an African American regiment that became known as the Buffalo Soldiers. The fort reconstruction provides a glimpse of what it was like to live and work at Fort Larned.

Fort Larned has a virtual tour which you can play from your phone or tablet. NPS recommends you watch before arriving; however, I also found it useful to play while standing in front of exhibits as well. It's like having your own tour guide walking around the site with you.

Fort Scott National Historic Site

Address: 1 Old Fort Blvd, Fort Scott, KS 66701

Phone: 620 223-0310

Website: https://www.nps.gov/fosc/index.htm

Overview: Congress established Fort Scott National Historic Site in 1978. It is located in southeastern Kansas, and NPS manages approximately 17 acres. Fort Scott was built in 1842 and was sold in 1845 which created the town of Fort Scott. In 1861, as the Civil War began, Fort Scott was reestablished as a military post. At the end of the Civil War, Fort Scott would close for its final time.
Fort Scott has a Virtual Tour using the NPS Fort Scott App available at the App Store and on Google Play. It is available for both phone and tablet.

Nicodemus National Historic Site

Address: 304 Washington Ave., Nicodemus, KS 67625

Phone: 785 839-4233

Website: https://www.nps.gov/nico/index.htm

Overview: Congress established Nicodemus National Historic Site in 1996 with approximately 161 acres. Nicodemus is a small rural town which had big hopes and dreams of becoming a thriving town. After the civil war, freed black slaves were not treated as equals. During the reconstruction period many black people from the east moved westward to Kansas. Nicodemus was the first town to be settled and built by African Americans in 1877. Five black ministers and a white developer created the town. In 1877, 300 settlers moved from Kentucky to start a new life and it flourished for a few years. There were several factors that led to the town almost disappearing, which included the railroad not going through the town and the Great Depression of 1930.

Stop at the Visitor Center to learn more about the town and its people. Take the walking tour around the small town to see some original architecture and visit some of the original churches. Many of the structures became National Historic Landmarks in 1976.

Tallgrass Prairie National Preserve

Address: 2480B KS Hwy 177, Strong City, KS 66869

Phone: 620 273-8494

Website: https://www.nps.gov/tapr/index.htm

Overview: Congress established the Tallgrass Prairie National Preserve with 10,894 acres in 1996. I had never been to a National Preserve and did not know what to expect. When I visited the Tallgrass Prairie National Preserve, I had envisioned only beautiful rolling hills of prairie grass. I was not even close. I was pleasantly surprised when I visited this site by gaining a better understanding of the families that came and lived on the tallgrass prairies. In addition to the beautiful landscape, you can visit the Spring HillZ bar ranch. The ranch is impressive, and it operated between 1878 and 1986.

The Tallgrass Prairie National Preserve has both guided and self-guided tours. Self-guided tours were easy to use and can be done at your own pace. Download the information to your phone or tablet and you don't even need an App. Use this link to start your tour: https://tapr.oncell.com/en/index.html

George Washington Carver National Monument

Address: 5646 Carver Road, Diamond, MO 64840

Phone: 417 325-4151

Website: https://www.nps.gov/gwca/index.htm

Overview: George Washington Carver National Monument was founded in 1943 with a $30,000 donation from Franklin Delano Roosevelt. The park is 240 acres and has a .75 mile nature trail.

George Washington Carver was born in approximately 1864, a slave on the Moses and Susan Carver farm. He took a keen interest in nature and studied plants and attended Simpson College in Iowa studying art. He then moved on to Iowa State Agriculture College (now Iowa State University) and completed his bachelor's degree in 1894, followed by his Master's in 1896. With his work on the value of peanuts, he became world famous. His testimony was crucial at the US Congress during the debate of the Emergency Tariff of 1921 bill.

I can't imagine how challenging it was for a young black man having to walk miles to go to school! And the discrimination against him. And even with all of those obstacles he was able to accomplish so many great things.

There is a hiking trail which guides you to historic sites such as his birthplace, view of Boy Carver Statue, Carver Spring, 1881 Moses Carver house, and the Carver Cemetery.

Harry S. Truman National Historic Site

Address: 223 North Main Street (Visitor Center), Independence, MO 64050

Phone: 816 254-2720

Website: https://www.nps.gov/hstr/index.htm

Overview: Harry S. Truman National Historic Site was founded in 1983. The park has about 10.5 acres and is located in the central part of western Missouri.

The site was the home of Harry S. Truman, the thirty-third president of the United States. At the site, take a guided tour by calling 816-254-9929 to verify that tours are available. Audio tours around the site are also available for your smartphone/cell phone at: http://myoncell.mobi/15856722611 or use the QR code.

You can also tour the Truman Farm at 12301 Blue Ridge Blvd. which is available year-round for self-guided tours. Visit the Nolan Home, one of Harry's cousins. And the home of the courtship of Bess, who would become his wife.

Ste. Genevieve National Historical Park

Address: 99 South Main Street, Ste. Genevieve, MO 63670

Phone: 573 880-7189

Website: https://www.nps.gov/stge/index.htm

Overview: This site was created as the National Historic Landmark District in 1960. In 2002, this site was added to the National Register of Historic Places. Then in 2020, it joined the National Park Service as Ste. Genevieve National Historical Park.

The site was the first permanent European settlement in Missouri and was established in 1750. The three features to visit include the Amoureux House, Jean Baptiste Valle House, and the Memorial Cemetery. The Amourex House is one of five structures in the United States that use poteaux-en-terre (post in ground) construction. The Jean Baptiste Valle House was named after political and military leader Ste. Genevieve. The Memorial Cemetery was built in 1787.

There are ranger guided tours of the Amoureux House and self-guided tours at the Jean Baptiste Valle Gardens. It is a relatively new park and service may be limited.

Ulysses S. Grant National Historic Site

Address: 7400 Grant Road, St. Louis, MO 63123

Phone: 314 842-1867

Website: https://www.nps.gov/ulsg/index.htm

Overview: Ulysses S. Grant National Historic Site became part of the National Park Service in 1989 and included approximately 9.7 acres of the original 850 acres of the White Haven Plantation.

Ulysses S. Grant was a Union commanding general during the Civil War. He later became the 18th president and served two terms (1869 to 1877).

This National Historic Site includes a Visitor Center, a separate museum, his main house, winter and summer kitchens, an ice house, a chicken house, and a walking tour.

Wilson's Creek National Battlefield

Address: 6424 W. Farm Road 182, Republic, MO 65738

Phone: 417 732-2662 x22

Website: https://www.nps.gov/wicr/index.htm

Overview: This battlefield is in the southwest portion of Missouri. It was added to the National Park Service in 1960 and to the National Register of Historic Places in 1966. There are approximately 1,750 acres within the park boundaries.

Wilson Creek battlefield is located about ten miles southwest of St. Louis, Missouri. It was the first battle of the Civil War fought in Missouri on August 10, 1861. Even though the losses were almost equal, the Union maintained control of Missouri throughout the war.

This site has a 4.9 mile road tour with eight interpretive stops pointing out significant events during the battle. There are five walking trails ranging from 1/4 to 3/4 of a mile each and an equestrian and hiking trail which is about 7 miles in length.

A Museum, Visitor Center, and an excellent Civil War research library is at the Wilson's Creek Visitor Center. Digital and virtual tours are available.

Agate Fossil Beds National Monument

Address: 301 River Road, Harrison, NE 69346

Phone: 308 665-4113

Website: https://www.nps.gov/agfo/index.htm

Overview: Agate Fossil Beds became a National Monument in 1997. It encompasses 3,058 acres in western Nebraska. There are two interpretive hiking trails, museum, and gift shop.

The Fossil Beds exploration began when James H. Cook settled in the Niobrara River area in 1874. There he met Chief Red Cloud, Oglala Lakota (Sioux), who thought that he was just another gold digger. After convincing Red Cloud that he was really a "bone hunter" they became good friends. In the museum you will see many of the gifts that Chief Red Cloud gave to James Cook in addition to skeletons of dinosaurs that roamed the area during the Cenozoic Era.

Fossil Hills Trail - This is the longer of the two trails and this one-way trail starts at the Visitor Center. The trail is paved with gentle slopes and at the end of the trail you will be rewarded with nice views. You will also see Carnegie Hill where, from 1904 to 1923, scientists from Yale University, the American Museum of National History, and others searched for dinosaurs that died in masses at this site.

Homestead National Monument of America

Address: 8523 West State Highway 4, Beatrice, NE

Phone: 402 223-3514

Website: https://www.nps.gov/home/index.htm

Overview: Homestead National Monument of America was established in 1936. There are approximately 211 acres to explore. As you can probably imagine, the monument was established for immigrants that arrived in the United States after the Civil War. Those venturous souls took the homesteading challenge and uncertainties of starting a new life on the western frontier. The westward expansion and the Homestead Act of 1862 opened up 270 million acres for that dream to become a reality.

Under the Homestead Act, the Government was giving away 160 acres of land and all you had to do was build a house, make improvements, and stay there for five years to obtain the title to the property. It wasn't easy as it sounds because you had to pick the plot of land from back east, sight unseen, pack up everything you own, move thousands of miles and build a house from whatever was on the land. Imagine, what would you do if you arrived at the badlands of South Dakota with limited water, very few trees, poor soil to grow crops, or raise livestock?

Did you know that homesteading was available in the lower 48 until 1976?

Did you know that homesteading was available in Alaska until 1988?

The Visitor Center is impressive with flags and interpretive boards that talk to each state's participation in the Homestead Act. Did you know that states in the east also had land available for homesteading?

Take the walk around the property and learn about the Freeman's homesteading story.

Visit the Native Plants Exhibit and Educational Center.

Scotts Bluff National Monument

Address: P.O. Box 27, Gering, NE

Phone: 308 436-9700

Website: https://www.nps.gov/scbl/index.htm

Overview: Scotts Bluff National Monument was created in 1919 and encompasses about 3,005 acres. It is located in the western part of the state.

While visiting Scotts Bluff National Monument you will experience the rugged terrain the early settlers had to deal with on the journey to California, Oregon, or Utah. At the monument you can take a 1.6 mile scenic drive up Summit Road to the top of Scotts Bluff. There are almost four miles of hiking trails to experience. The Saddle Rock Trail will take you to the top of Scotts Bluff, but my favorite is the actual trail where the wagons traveled; you can see the ruts from the wheels. Bicycling is very popular at this park with rides down the Prairie View Trail and the Summit Road, when it is closed to automobiles (prior to the road opening or after is closes at the end of the day).

The following is a list of Historic Trails, recreation areas, and historic rivers.

California National Historic Trail
CA, CO, ID, KS, MO, NE, NV, OR, UT, WY

Address: PO Box 728, Santa Fe, NM, 87504
Phone: 505 988-6098
Website: https://www.nps.gov/cali/index.htm

Overview: Follow in the footsteps of over 250,000 emigrants who traveled to the gold fields and rich farmlands of California during the 1840s and 1850s, the greatest mass migration in American history. The California National Historic Trail is over 5,000 miles long and covers portions of 10 states. Step into history along more than 1,000 miles of ruts and traces from travelers and their overland wagons. Source: NPS

Lewis & Clark National Historic Trail
IA, ID, IL, IN, KS, KY, MO, MT, NE, ND, OH, OR, PA, SD, WA, WV

Address: 601 Riverfront Drive, Omaha, NE, 68102
Phone: 402 661-1804
Website: https://www.nps.gov/lecl/index.htm

Overview: The Lewis and Clark National Historic Trail is approximately 4,900 miles long, extending from Pittsburgh, Pennsylvania, to the mouth of the Columbia River, near present day Astoria, Oregon. It follows the historic outbound and inbound routes of the Lewis and Clark Expedition as well as the preparatory section from Pittsburgh, Pennsylvania to Wood River, Illinois. Source: NPS

Missouri National Recreational River
Yankton, SD, NE

Address: 508 East 2nd Street, Yankton, SD, 57078
Phone: 605 665-0209 X28
Website: https://www.nps.gov/mnrr/index.htm

Overview: Imagine a 100-mile stretch of North America's longest river, a vestige of the untamed American West. The Missouri National Recreational River is where imagination meets reality. Two free flowing stretches of the Missouri make up the National Park. Relive the past by making an exploration of the wild, untamed and mighty river that continues to flow as nature intended. Source: NPS

Mormon Pioneer National Historic Trail
IL, IA, NE, UT, WY

Address: PO Box 728, Santa Fe, MM, 87504
Phone: 505 988-6098
Website: https://www.nps.gov/mopi/index.htm

Overview: Explore the Mormon Pioneer National Historic Trail across five states to see the 1,300-mile route traveled by Mormons who fled Nauvoo, Illinois, to the Great Salt Lake Valley in 1846-1847. Source: NPS

Niobrara National Scenic River
Valentine, NE

Address: 214 W US Highway 20, Valentine, NE, 69201
Phone: 402 376-1901
Website: https://www.nps.gov/niob/index.htm

Overview: With a little something for everyone, the Niobrara National Scenic River is a destination for crossing adventures off your bucket list. Most popular for river recreation, you can float the Niobrara River on a canoe, tube, or kayak as a beginner and have a blast. Hiking, biking, and wildlife watching keep our visitors busy. Oh! And we haven't even told you about the waterfalls yet. Source: NPS

Oregon National Historic Trail
ID, KS, MO, NE, OR, WA, WY

Address: PO Box 728, Santa Fe, MM, 87504
Phone: 505 988-6098
Website: https://www.nps.gov/oreg/index.htm

Overview: Imagine yourself an emigrant headed for Oregon: would promises of lush farmlands and a new beginning lure you to leave home and walk for weeks? More than 2,000 miles of trail ruts and traces can still be seen along the Oregon National Historic Trail in six states and serve as reminders of the sacrifices, struggles, and triumphs of early American settlers. Source: NPS

Pony Express National Historic Trail
CA, CO, KS, MO, NE, NV, UT, WY

Address: PO Box 728, Santa Fe, MM, 87504
Phone: 505 988-6098
Website: https://www.nps.gov/poex/index.htm

Overview: It is hard to believe that young men once rode horses to carry mail from Missouri to California in the unprecedented time of only 10 days. This relay system along the Pony Express National Historic Trail in eight states was the most direct and practical means of east-west communications before the telegraph. Source: NPS

Trail Of Tears National Historic Trail
AL, AR, GA, IL, KY, MO, NC, OK, TN

Address: PO Box 728, Santa Fe, MM, 87504
Phone: 505 988-6098
Website: https://www.nps.gov/trte/index.htm

Overview: Remember and commemorate the survival of the Cherokee people, forcefully removed from their homelands in Georgia, Alabama, and Tennessee to live in Indian Territory, now Oklahoma. They traveled by foot, horse, wagon, or steamboat in 1838-1839. Source: NPS

8 INDIANA DUNE OVERVIEW

Indiana Dunes National Lakeshore was established in 1966 and in 2019, the US Congress designated it as the 61st National Park with approximately 15,000 acres. It is located in the northwestern part of Indiana on Lake Michigan and was visited by 2,134,285 people in 2019.

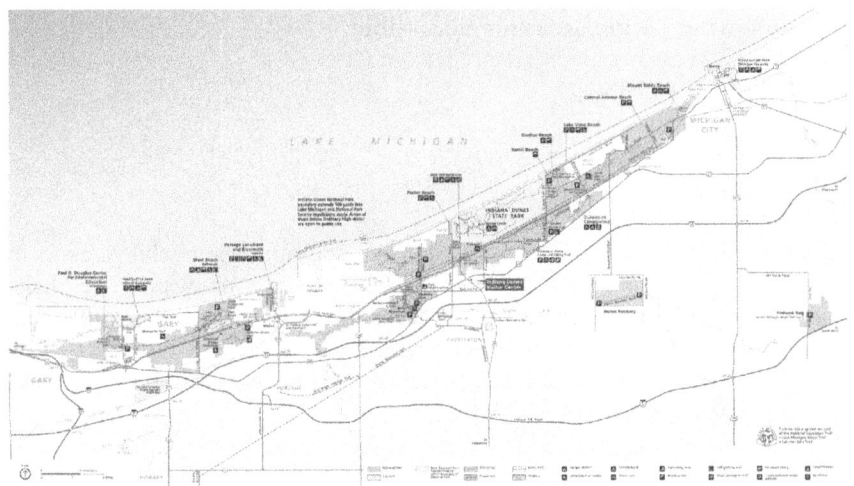

Contact Information: 1100 North Mineral Springs Road Porter, IN 46304

Website: https://www.nps.gov/indu/index.htm

Physical Address: 1100 North Mineral Springs Road Porter, IN 46304

Phone: 219 395-1882

GPS Coordinates:
Northeast entrance: N41°41'56.2" W86°55'57.3"
South Visitor Center: N41°37'37.4" W87°05'09.9"
West entrance: N41°37'08.9" W87°09'11.0"

ADA Accessibility:
Major sites within the park that are accessible with assistance include:

- Indiana Dunes National Park Visitor Center (building, displays, and hearing assist device for the theater).

- Paul H. Douglas Center for Environmental Education (building and displays).
- Portage Lakefront and Riverwalk (paved hiking trail, pavilion, and fishing pier).
- Dunewood Campground (sites 15, 30, 41 and 55).

Accessible parking and restroom services are available throughout the park. A standard wheelchair is available for loan at the Paul H. Douglas Center.

The following picnic areas are accessible:
- West Beach
- Bailly Chellberg
- Tremont
- Glenwood Dunes
- Lake View Beach
- Tolleston Dunes Overlook
- Indiana Dunes National Park has made significant achievements in providing access to beach areas. Access to waters of Lake Michigan pose challenging accessibility problems. The following beach areas have limited accessibility:
- West Beach (a beach wheelchair can be checked out from the lifeguards).
- Lake View (the picnic shelters and overlook are accessible).

A good place to look for the latest information on accessibility is the Disabled Traveler's Companion. Website: http://www.tdtcompanion.com.
While not officially affiliated with the National Park Service, they have been working with Indiana Dunes National Lakeshore and other National Parks to provide valuable information to the disabled traveler. Their website contains information on, and photographs of, campgrounds, lodges, and park attractions that will aid in planning your trip to Indiana Dunes National Lakeshore.

Source: NPS

Birdwatching
352 various species

Mammals
41 various species

Plants
1,130 various species

Web cameras: https://www.nps.gov/grsa/learn/photosmultimedia/webcams.htm

When do most visitors visit Indiana Dunes National Park?
This will give you a good overview of the attendance based on monthly totals for 2019.

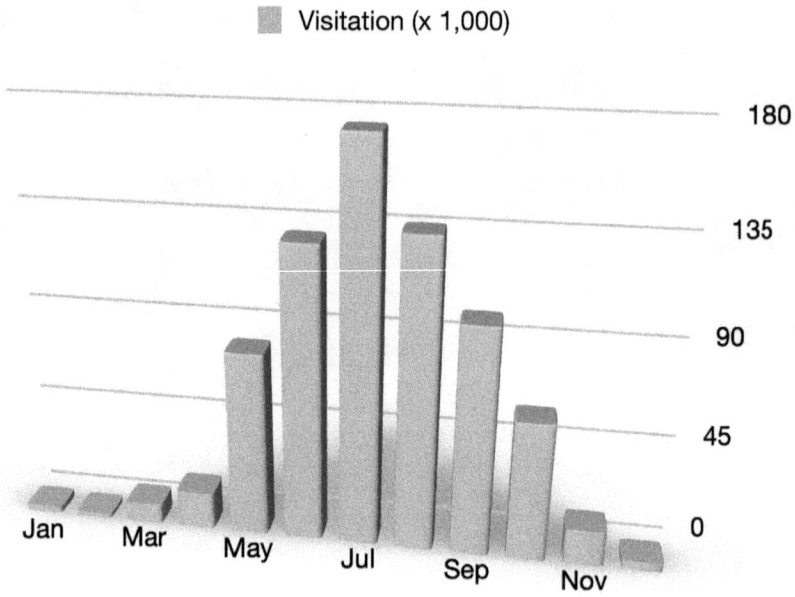

Source: NationalParkPlanningGuides.com

Historical Precipitation

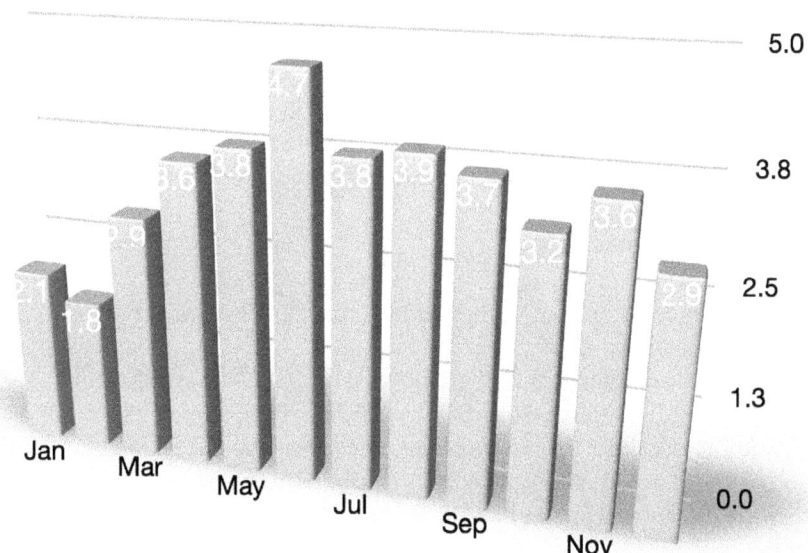

Historical Temperature

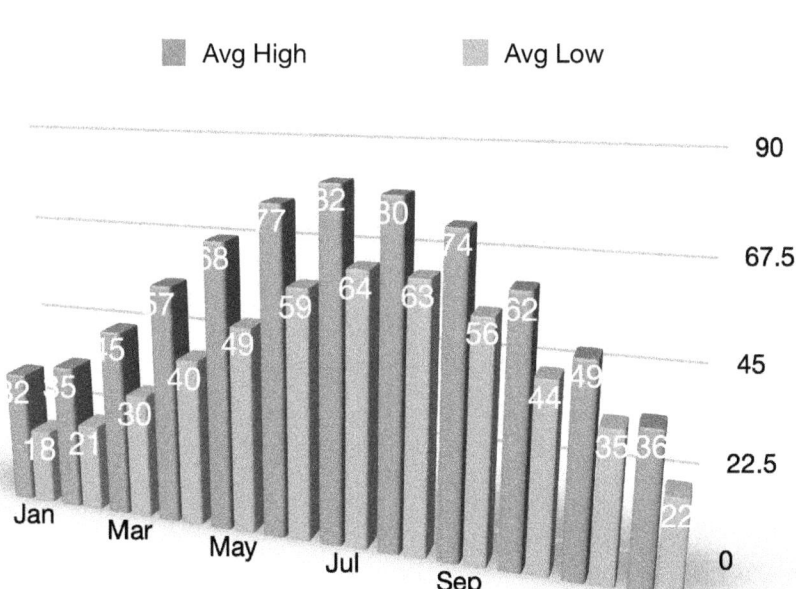

9 INDIANA DUNE HISTORY

Residential Development, 1870 to 1970 - Most of the residential houses and factories appeared over time due to its recreational value and location so close to Chicago, IL. As you look around, you will notice as you hike on trails and drive around the park you are always within sight or sound of the steel mills, factories, commercial businesses, and housing developments.

Park History Timeline:

- 1916 Director Steven Mather had hearings in Chicago for a "Sand Dunes National Park"
- 1926 Indiana Dunes State Park opened
- 1966 Congress authorized the protection of the national lakeshore and the port and created Indiana Dunes National Lakeshore.
- 2019 as part of the Consolidated Appropriations Act of 2019, the Indiana Dunes National Park was created.

10 INDIANA DUNE ACTIVITIES

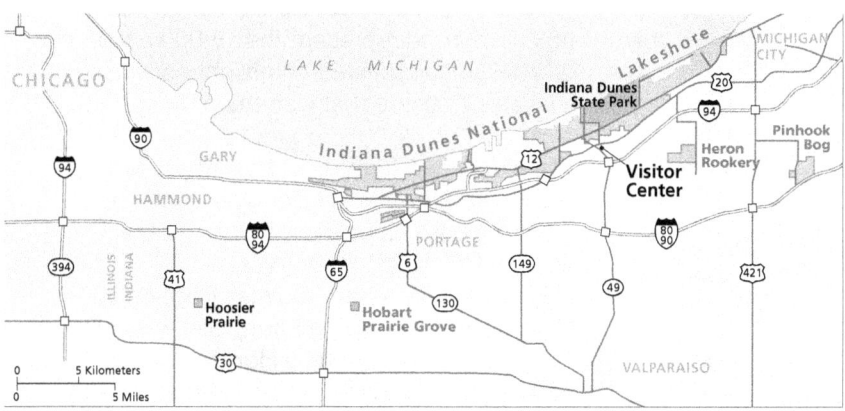

National Park Scheduled Events

Every National Park has a Junior Ranger Program. You probably have seen or been the one that is working with their children completing the program. More and more adults are also becoming Junior Rangers and at some sites they even have a 'Not So Junior Ranger' Badge or a 'Senior Ranger' Badge. The information in the books is top notch. Yellowstone was my first badge, and I was impressed with the quality and content of the material and it was fun too.

Calendar of events: https://www.nps.gov/indu/planyourvisit/calendar.htm

	Time	Description
Special Exhibit Celebrating the 61st National Park	30 minutes	The 6,500-square-foot exhibit hall will be transformed to represent the 15,000 acres of diverse landscapes and highlight activities available to those that visit the park system. The exhibit will feature 12 trail stops: Miller Woods and the Paul H Douglas Center for Environmental Education, Hobart Prairie Grove and Little Calumet River, West Beach, Portage Lakefront & Riverwalk, Cowles Bog, Bailly Homestead / Chellberg Farm, Glenwood Dunes Trail, Century of Progress Homes, Indiana Dunes State Park, Dunewood Campground, Mount Baldy, and Pinhook Bog. There will be interactive exhibits for children along the trail, selfie stations and a large "sandbox" for building sandcastles.
Beachside with a Ranger	4 hours	Stop by and learn about our park's preservation story. We'll highlight some of the challenges the region faced in the past as well as the largest threats that confront us today.
Drop-in Volunteering at West Beach	1 hour	Join staff and fellow volunteers in helping to care for your local national park. Wear comfortable clothes; work gloves and equipment will be provided.
Biking & Birding	3 hours	Bring your bike and we will provide the binoculars and take you to some fun spots in Miller to see birds and enjoy a morning bike ride. Get your exercise and learn some basic birding techniques.

	Time	Description
Lake Michigan Boat Tour	2 hours	Adult: $30 Children (Ages 3-11): $16 Infant (3 or Younger): Free Join us Saturday mornings on our Riding with a Ranger Tour led by the Indiana Dunes National Park Rangers. This 2 hour tour will be filled with fun and facts for the whole family. Tour starts in Michigan City and follows the shoreline of the National Park out and back. Be sure to book your reservations at www.harborcountryadventures.com beforehand.
Pinhook Bog Open House	3 hours	You can tour the bog on your own and you can talk to rangers stationed along the trail who will help you understand this unique place filled with carnivorous plants. Please arrive by 2:00 pm to allow about one hour to walk the trail and tour the bog. RESERVATION OR REGISTRATION: YES
Playdate in the Nature Play Zone	2 hours	Kids of all ages are invited to spend a couple of hours having fun in nature at Indiana Dunes National Park. Join a ranger at the Paul H Douglas Center for Environmental Education's Nature Play Zone to build a fort, climb a tree, create awesome nature art, or just have fun exploring nature.
Science in the National Park	2 hours	Meet local experts and scientists who are conducting research in the national park. Examine the knowledge gained by researchers during a presentation on their work and a short hike afterward.

	Time	Description
Mount Baldy Open House	3 hours	Explore the issues and science around the park's largest living dune. Drop by the Mt. Baldy parking lot to talk with park staff and enjoy hands on activities. The dune is still closed for general public use. We strongly ask the public to respect and follow posted closure signs and stay out of roped-off areas. The dune is still closed for reasons of public safety and restoration efforts.
Miller Woods Hike on the Paul H. Douglas Trail	2 hours	Join a park ranger for a hike through the beautiful oak savanna of Indiana Dunes National Park's Miller Woods. Hikes will vary in length depending on the interest and abilities of visitors. This ranger-led hike starts at the Paul H. Douglas Center and continues through Miller Woods to the shore of Lake Michigan. This amazing hike goes through a globally rare black oak savanna and around towering sand dunes and interdunal wetlands. Wear sturdy shoes, bring water, and insect repellent.
Feeding Time at Chellberg Farm	30 minutes	Join a ranger and help us feed the farm animals.
Art in the National Park	2 hours	Join a local artist and learn how to paint the dunes every second Saturday of the month at Portage Lakefront and Riverwalk in Indiana Dunes National Park. The Art Barn is providing an artist to teach visitors how to paint a picture inspired by the dunes. A canvas and paint will be provided for this free class. Registration is required and the class is limited to 20 adult painters.

	Time	Description
Music Heritage Series Concert	1 hour 30 minutes	The Save the Tunes Council is a group of local musicians devoted to preserving and passing on folk songs in the traditional way, using a variety of musical instruments including guitar, autoharp, dulcimer, banjo, harmonica, bagpipe, penny whistle, hurdy gurdy, and other obscure instruments.
Apple Festival 2019	5 hours	This family-friendly event features seasonal activities such as free, tractor-pulled hayrides, a Kid's Corner with games and crafts, and even apple-chucking catapults. You can help make cider using an apple press, learn how to cook apples for applesauce and apple butter, ferment apples into vinegar, make apple pomanders and discover dozens of other uses for apples. Free tasting of most of these products will be available. Or, purchase apples, lunch or a snack from one of several food vendors and a farm stand market featuring local produce. Enjoy your treats while listening to local musicians on stage and the Northwest Indiana Storytellers.
Century of Progress House Talk	2 hours	FEE: $10 for this talk ($5 for members of Indiana Landmarks and Dunes National Park Association) The house tours last a little over two hours and are guided by park rangers and volunteers who will provide histories and architectural overviews at each property. The tour admits visitors to the first floor of the restored Florida Tropical, Rostone, Armco-Ferro and Cypress houses. Also on the tour is the House of Tomorrow, declared a National Treasure by the National Trust for Historic Preservation, but still in need of restoration. Indiana Landmarks is currently accepting proposals for the property's restoration and long-term lease.

	Time	Description
Birding with the Indiana Audubon Society	2 hours	Join birding expert and Indiana Audubon Society Executive Director Brad Bumgardner on for his monthly Indiana Dunes birding series. RESERVATION OR REGISTRATION: YES
Stargazing Through Telescopes	2 hours	Join members from the Chicago Astronomical Society, Michiana Astronomical Society, and Calumet Astronomical Society with their telescopes as they introduce the night skies to visitors at the Indiana Dunes National Park's Kemil Beach parking lot. The experts will train their massive telescopes on interesting features and discuss the incredible night sky. Please dress for the weather as there is no indoor space at the Kemil beach parking lot. It may be helpful to bring a pair of binoculars from home.

Source: NPS

Hiking

Paper trail maps are available at the Indiana Dunes Visitor Center and at each trailhead kiosk (note: not at the trailheads that we went to), or better yet save a tree by using the REI Co-Op National Parks guide for hiking maps for each National Park which provides a huge amount of information. If you want paper, I would print off the trails that you plan to hike ahead of time.

Bailly Homestead, Chellberg Farm, Little Calumet River and Mnoké Prairie Trail System	Easy to moderate 3.4 mi/ zz km average 2 hrs.	Yes	Hike through a forest dominated by maple, beech, basswood and oak trees. Follow a stretch of the Little Calumet River and explore the recently restored Mnoké Prairie. Explore the historic Bailly Homestead and Chellberg Farm.

Calumet Dunes Trail System	Easy 0.5 miles in average 20 mins.	Yes	This short, wheelchair accessible, paved trail features the Calumet Dunes ridge that formed at what once was the edge of the Lake Michigan over 12,000 years ago.
Cowles Bog Trail System	Moderate to strenuous 4.7 miles in average 4 hours	Yes	This trail highlights an area of such outstanding plant diversity that it was designated as a National Natural Landmark. Explore several distinct habitats including ponds, marshes, swamps, black oak savannas and beaches.
Dune Ridge Trail System	Moderate 0.7 miles average 30 mins.	Yes	This trail offers great views of the extensive wetlands and forests south of this tall, forested dune. Perhaps no other area in the national park will take you through as many diverse habitats in such a short trail.
Glenwood Dunes Trail System	Moderate, 6.8 miles in length, average hike time of 4 hours	No in the horse are a	This extensive trail system features interconnected loops in mature woods ranging from less than a mile to nearly 15 miles and is popular with hikers, runners, horseback riders and cross-country skiers.
Great Marsh Trail System	Easy, 1.7 miles in length, average hike time of 1 hour	Yes	A really nice birding hike with views of the largest wetland complex in the Lake Michigan watershed. Features a separate wheelchair accessible paved trail with quick access to an observation deck.
Heron Rookery Trail System	Easy, 3.3 miles in length, average hike time of 2 hours	Yes	This trail follows a portion of the Little Calumet River. In the spring, the woodlands along this trail are blanketed with the most extensive display of spring wildflowers in the national park.

Hobart Prairie Grove Trail System (Hobart Woodland)	Easy, 2.2 miles in length, average hike time of 1 hour	Yes	This hike has views of forested ravines, bur oak savanna, and scenic Lake George.
Hobart Prairie Grove Trail System (Oak Savannah)	3.9 miles in length, average hike time of 2 hours.	Yes	This rail trail offers scenic views of Lake George and mature forests and is great for biking and hiking.
Pinhook Trail System (Upland Hike)	Moderate, 2.1 miles in length, average hike time of 1.5 hours	Yes	The Upland Trail highlights a rich beech and maple forest growing on top of a glacial moraine formed about 15,000 years ago. The Upland Hike is open to the public year round without the need for a guided tour.
Pinhook Trail System (Bog Hike)	Easy, 0.9 miles in length, average hike time of 1 hour	No	The Bog Trail leads to a bog in a depression in the moraine created when a large piece of ice broke off the melting glacier. The bog features an incredible habitat with unique plants. ***Restricted Access.** Access to Pinhook Bog requires advance approval and accompaniment by authorized staff. There are ranger-led open houses on weekends in the summer. Program dates and times can be obtained by calling the Indiana Dunes Visitor Center at (219) 395-1882.

Portage Lakefront and Riverwalk	Easy, 1.5 miles in length, average hike time of 45 minutes	Yes	This popular location is a great place to view the ever-changing seasons along Lake Michigan and watch dramatic weather and clouds build over the lake. It's an easy location to watch for migrating birds in the spring and summer, and observe shelf ice that forms along the beach edge in the winter.
Tolleston Dunes Trail System	Moderate, 2.9 miles in length, average hike time of 2 hours	Yes	This trail winds amid varied habitats ranging from oak savanna to wetlands and plants such as prickly pear cactus, butterfly weed and lupines. Features a separate wheelchair accessible trail with quick access to an observation deck with picnic tables.
West Beach Trail System (3-Loop)	Moderate to rugged, 3.5 miles in length, average hike time of 3 hours	Yes	These trails offer a great combination of hiking and relaxing at the beach. The trails are varied and encompass many habitats. There are great views from the top of the Dune Succession Trail stairs, a beautiful pinery of jack pines, birding opportunities along Long Lake and secluded sections of forest.
West Beach Trail System (Dunes Succession)	Moderate, 1.0 mile in length, average hike time of 45 minutes.	Yes	These trails offer a great combination of hiking and relaxing at the beach. The trails are varied and encompass many habitats. There are great views from the top of the Dune Succession Trail stairs, a beautiful pinery of jack pines, birding opportunities along Long Lake and secluded sections of forest.

Backcountry Camping

There is no backcountry camping available at Indiana Dunes National Park.

Beach-going and Swimming

https://www.nps.gov/indu/planyourvisit/swimming.htm

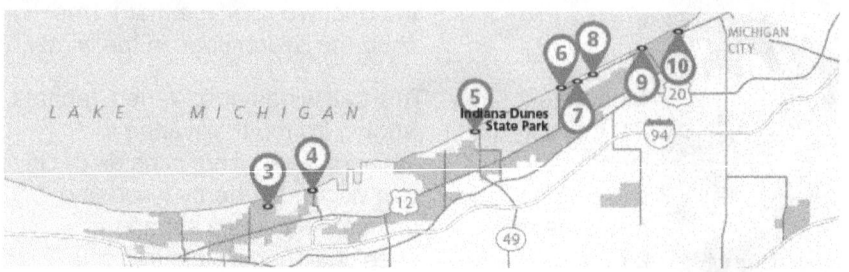

If you like to spend time at the beach, Indiana offers approximately fifteen miles of shoreline to enjoy along Lake Michigan. Listed below are some of the beaches in the park.

- 3. West Beach - Parking fees (amenity fee) are charged per vehicle.
- 4. Portage Lakefront and Riverwalk Beach
- 5. Porter Beach
- 6. Kemil Beach
- 7. Dunbar Beach
- 8. Lake View Beach
- 9. Central Avenue Beach
- 10. Mount Baldy Beach (Beach is open, DUNE IS CLOSED)

Beach FREE Shuttle
https://www.nps.gov/indu/planyourvisit/indu_dune_buggy_shuttle.htm

The park service offers FREE park shuttles to Kemil and Lake Street beaches and Marquette Park. They operate both Eastern and Western shuttle bus routes between the Friday of Memorial Day to Labor Day.

Eastern Route
Hours: 10:00 am - 6:00 pm *

Shuttle runs every 20 - 30 minutes
* Note: no shuttle run from 2:00 pm - 2:30 pm

Stop Locations:
- Dunewood Campground
- USGS Great Lakes Research Center
- Kemil Beach Parking Lot

Western Route
Hours: 10:00 am - 6:00 pm *

Shuttle runs every 20 - 30 minutes
* Note: no shuttle run from 2:00 pm - 2:30 pm

Stop Locations:
- Miller Train Station
- Marquette Park
- Douglas Center
- 5th Avenue and Lake Street
- Lake Street Beach

Bicycles

Bicycle usage in Indiana Dunes National Park is not limited to just the public roads. There are 37 miles of trails inside park. Download the national parks interactive trail guide phone.

Apple: https://apps.apple.com/us/app/rei-national-parks-guide-maps/id1031987936

or Android: https://play.google.com/store/apps/details?id=com.adventureprojects.nationalparks&hl=en

- Not in park - Dunes Kankakee Trail Paved, 3.6 miles round trip, paved, paralleling US 49 from the National Park Visitor Center to the entrance of State Park entrance. It is mostly flat with the exceptions of the overpasses at US Routes 12 and 20.

- https://www.nps.gov/indu/planyourvisit/dunes-kankakee.htm

- Not in the park - Prairie Duneland Trail The trail is located outside the park and is paved, 22.4 miles round trip, rail trail, flat.

- https://www.nps.gov/indu/planyourvisit/prairie-duneland.htm

- 24 - Porter Brickyard Trail Is listed as paved, 7.0 miles round trip, some hills. The trail was just OK. On the trail you will pass the rear of park headquarters and maintenance area.

- https://www.nps.gov/indu/planyourvisit/porter-brickyard.htm

- 25 - Calumet Trail Gravel service road that runs adjacent to the railroad tracks, 19.0 miles round trip, flat.

- https://www.nps.gov/indu/planyourvisit/calumet.htm

- 26 - Marquette Trail. Paved 4.6 miles round trip, rail trail, flat. The trail was once the railroad bed for the Harbor Belt Railroad.

- https://www.nps.gov/indu/planyourvisit/marquette.htm

- 27 - Oak Savannah Trail Paved The trail is located outside of the park and is 17.8 miles round trip, a rail trail, and flat.

- https://www.nps.gov/indu/planyourvisit/oak-savannah.htm

Bird Watching Festival

Indiana Dunes Birding Festival is held the third weekend in May.

Boating

There are no marinas, boat rentals, or boat launches within the park. Facilities are available outside the park at:

- Porter County: www.indianadunes.com
- Lake County: www.southshorecva.com
- LaPorte County: www.michigancitylaporte.com

Launching kayaks in the park is permitted, except at West Beach's swimming area.

Cross country skiing/ Snowshoeing

Cross-country skiing and snowshoeing are two great activities at Indiana Dunes National Park. The park does not offer rental equipment. Trails are not groomed, and the park recommends calling the Visitor Center at (219) 395-1882 for trail conditions. The two areas are:

- The Glenwood Dunes Trail System offers 15 miles of trails of gentle rolling dunes.
- Tolleston Dunes Trail System offers more variety for the advanced skiers.

For additional information:
https://www.nps.gov/indu/planyourvisit/winteractivities.htm

Fishing

Fishing requires an Indiana Fishing License and a stamp f0r fishing for trout or salmon.

https://www.nps.gov/indu/planyourvisit/fishing-and-boating.htm

Geocaching

Want to do an activity while you are out hiking? Try geocaching…. Using the Geocaching App at: https://www.geocaching.com/play, or use GPS or phone with a GPS, to search for cache sites with hidden containers. Indiana Dunes is just starting this, with the promise of more to come. See the link below:

https://www.nps.gov/indu/planyourvisit/indiana-dunes-geocaching.htm

Here is the first location and things to solve…

> **Chellberg Farm / Bailly Homestead Trail System:**
> GPS Coordinates (N 41° 37' 29", W 87° 05' 22")
> Geocache Sites...
> #1 What's Our Grade?
> #2 Identify a Sugar Maple Tree.
> #3 What's Wrong with the Collection Site?
> #4 Can Trees Really Move?

Hiking Trails

Paper trail maps are available at the Indiana Dunes Visitor Center and at each trailhead kiosk (Note: We found that maps weren't available at all trailheads.). Another alternative would be to use the REI Co-Op National Parks guide for hiking maps (https://www.hikingproject.com/nationalparks). Available for each National Park and provides a huge amount of information. If you want paper, it can be printed for the trails you plan to hike.

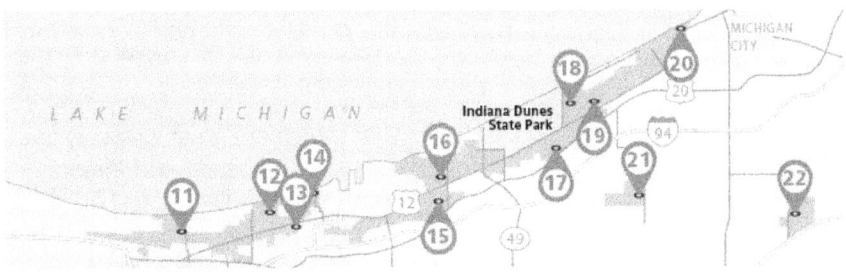

	Name	Difficulty	Distance Round Trip	Description
15	Bailly Homstead Chellberg Farm Trail	Easy/Moderate	3.4 mi / 5.6 km, 2 hours average hike time	Hike through a forest dominated by maple, beech, basswood and oak trees. Follow a stretch of the Little Calumet River and explore the recently restored Mnoké Prairie. Explore the historic Bailly Homestead and Chellberg Farm.
25	Calumet Dunes Trail	Easy	0.5 mi / 0.8 km, 20 minutes average hike time	This short, wheelchair accessible, paved trail features the Calumet Dunes ridge that formed at what once was the edge of the Lake Michigan over 12,000 years ago.

	Name	Difficulty	Distance Round Trip	Description
16	Cowles Bog Trail	Moderate/ Strenuous	4.7 mi / 7.6 km, 4 hours average hike time	This trail highlights an area of such outstanding plant diversity that it was designated as a National Natural Landmark. Explore several distinct habitats including ponds, marshes, swamps, black oak savannas and beaches.
18	Dune Ridge Trail	Moderate	0.7 mi / 1.1 km, 30 minutes average hike time	This trail offers great views of the extensive wetlands and forests south of this tall, forested dune. Perhaps no other area in the national park will take you through as many diverse habitats in such a short trail.
17	Glenwood Dunes Trail	Moderate	6.8 mi / 10.9 km, 4 hour average hike time	This extensive trail system features interconnected loops in mature woods ranging from less than a mile to nearly 15 miles and is popular with hikers, runners, horseback riders and cross-country skiers.
19	Great Marsh Trail	Easy	1.7 mi / 2.7 km, 1 hour average hike time	A really nice birding hike with views of the largest wetland complex in the Lake Michigan watershed. Features a separate wheelchair accessible paved trail with quick access to an observation deck.
21	Heron Rookery Trail	Easy	3.3 mi / 5.3 km, 2 hours average hike time	This trail follows a portion of the Little Calumet River. In the spring, the woodlands along this trail are blanketed with the most extensive display of spring wildflowers in the national park.

	Name	Difficulty	Distance Round Trip	Description
None	Hobart Prairie Grove Trail	Easy	2.2 mi / 3.5 km, 1 hour average hike time	This hike has views of forested ravines, bur oak savanna, and scenic Lake George.
None	Old Savana Trail	Easy	3.9 mi / 6.3 km, 2 hours average hike time	This rail trail offers scenic views of Lake George and mature forests and is great for biking and hiking.
11	Paul H. Douglas Trail (Miller Woods)	Moderate	3.4 mi / 5.6 km, 2.5 hour average hike time	This trail winds through several habitats including wetlands, globally rare black oak savanna, open dunes and beach. The views of the lake and the dunes are incredible.
10	Mount Baldy Trail	Strenuous	0.8 mi / 1.3 km, 1 hour average hike time	This hike is short with a steep climb up loose sand to reach the top of Mount Baldy. The views are incredible as you hike on top of the barren (or bald) sand dune.
22	Pinhook Trail Upland Hike	Moderate	2.1 mi / z.z km, 1.5 hours average hike time	The Upland Trail highlights a rich beech and maple forest growing on top of a glacial moraine formed about 15,000 years ago. The Upland Hike is open to the public year round without the need for a guided tour.

	Name	Difficulty	Distance Round Trip	Description
22	Pinhook Trail Bog Hike Trail	Easy	0.9 mi / 1.4 km, 1 hour average hike time	The Bog Trail leads to a bog in a depression in the moraine created when a large piece of ice broke off the melting glacier. The bog features an incredible habitat with unique plants.
14	Portage Lakefront and Riverwalk	Easy	1.5 mi / 2.4 km, 45 minutes average hike time	This loop combines the Jones Creek Trail, the Lower Talkington Trail, and the Lower Paddock Creek Trail. Add it to the Upper Paddock/Talkington Loop for an epic adventure of 23.4 miles.
13	Tolleston Dunes Trail	Moderate	2.9 mi / 4.7 km, 2 hours average hike time	This trail combines part of the Lower Talkington Trail with the Upper Talkington and Upper Paddock Creek Trails. Accessing the loop from Painted Canyon will add 4 miles round trip to your hike.
12	West Beach Trail 3-Loop Hike	Moderate/ Strenuous	3.5 mi / 5.6 km, 3 hours average hike time	

Name	Difficulty	Distance Round Trip	Description
12 West Beach Trail Dunes Succession Hike	Moderate	1.0 mi / 1.6 km, 45 minutes average hike time	These trails offer a great combination of hiking and relaxing at the beach. The trails are varied and encompass many habitats. There are great views from the top of the Dune Succession Trail stairs, a beautiful pinery of jack pines, birding opportunities along Long Lake and secluded sections of forest.

Historical Sites

Bailly Homestead

This site was the home of Joseph Bailly, an early homesteader to northern Indiana. In addition to being an independent fur trader, his trading post provided supplies to locals and a place to stay for those that were traveling westward.

Chellberg Farm

The Chellberg Farm was owned and operated by Swedish immigrants Anders and Johanna Chellberg. The property was in the family for three generations. Take a tour of the grounds and enjoy the beauty where they once lived.

Houses of the Future

These are a one-of-a-kind attraction and only exist at this national park. There are five houses which were entered into a contest at the 1923 World's Fair. The modern house designs were way ahead of their time. The design criteria for the World's Fair Houses of the Future Contest was 'It could be massed produced and affordable'.

The houses are still in use today and some can be rented out, but I imagine it would be very expensive.

House of Tomorrow

The house of tomorrow has a first-floor garage and airplane hangar, which in 1933 was photographed with a biplane. The second and third floor are of steel construction with walls of mainly glass. The use of glass walls defied mechanical engineering principals of the time. As it turned out the glass windows and "curtain wall system" turned out to be very efficient.

Florida Tropical House

The Florida Tropical House is a two-story construction with large balconies and roof terrace for entertaining. The design is traditional stucco outside walls and are painted flamingo pink (our house in Hollywood, Florida was also pink in the 1960s).

Armco-Ferro House

It is the only remaining house that met the design criteria. The construction was simple utilizing corrugated steel panels that were interchangeable. This design was used after World War II to build what we know today as a prefab home.

Cypress Log Cabin

The Cypress Log Cabin construction was meant to show the many uses of the Cypress tree in the construction of a beautiful mountain lodge setting.

Wieboldt-Rostone House

The Wiebolt-Rostone House is a contemporary structure built using a steel frame clad with Rostone. Rostone was a new technique which attached shale, limestone, and alkali to the steel. Unfortunately, the concept of Rostone did not stand up over the years. Most of the Rostone was replaced with Perma-stone, but the park service states Rostone remains "surrounding the front door exterior, in the interior entrance area, and around the living room fireplace".

Horseback Riding

There are no guided trail rides at Indiana Dunes National Park. However, if you have a horse, horseback riding is permitted on the Glenwood Dunes Trail. Additional information for horse use and riding in the park is here: https://www.nps.gov/indu/planyourvisit/horse.htm

Glenwood Dunes Equestrian Trail - Is the only equestrian trail in the park. Rides can range from less than a mile to almost 15 miles depending on the interconnecting trails that you take.

Indiana Dunes State Park

Indiana Dunes State Park has 2,182 acres to explore. The state park is nestled within the National Park and offers unique opportunities for camping, hiking, and exploring more of the Indiana Dunes.

The state park was established in 1925 and has some of the more spectacular dunes.

Activities at Indiana Dunes State Park
- Nature Center/Interpretive Naturalist service
- Picnicking/Shelters
- Access to Calumet trail (connects to the National Park)
- Fishing
- Three Dune Hiking Challenge (If you only do one hike in the state park, this is the one that I would highly recommend).
- Swimming
- Birding
- Biking

Camping

The state park has 140 beautiful sites with 50 amp service.

For reservations: https://indianastateparks.reserveamerica.com

Things to do outside the park

Fishing

Fishing on Lake Michigan is good; springtime fish for bass, bluegill, salmon, and trout. In the summer, you can fish for yellow perch near the shore.

Golfing

	Phone	Website
The Braasie Golf Club	219 921-1192	
Michigan City Municipal Golf Course - North	219 873-1517	
Michigan City Golf Course	219 873-1516	https://www.michigancitygolfcourse.com
Robbinhurst Golf Club & Driving Range	219 762-9711	
Forest Park Golf Course	219 531-7888	
Sand Creek Country Club	219 395-5200	

Museums

	Phone	Website
Barker Mansion	219 873-1520	
The Depot - Beverly Shores History Museum & Art Gallery	219 874-8000	

	Phone	Website
Old Lighthouse Museum	219 872-6133	
Westchester Public Library - Township History Museum	219 983-9715	

11 INDIANA DUNE PERSONAL FAVORITES

Bailly Homestead

This site was the home of Joseph Bailly and his family. The big house was beautiful but was not open for viewing when we visited the park. The log cabin looks like it would have been cozy too.

BARK Ranger Program

Indiana Dunes has a great BARK Ranger Program and it is free. To get my really cool Bark Ranger dog tag here is what I had to do.

Bag my waste (make sure my parents bag and properly dispose of my waste)

Alway wear a leash (I will wear a leash no more than 6 feet/ 2 meters long)

Respect wildlife (I will not bark or chase wildlife)

Know where I can go (I will make sure that my parents do not go where they don't belong)

Beaches

West Beach is the largest beach area and can accommodate 655 cars and 50 oversized vehicles. They have a huge pavilion with restrooms, food and beverage area, and even a place to get out of the sun for awhile.

Biking

Indiana Dunes is a great place for mountain biking since the trails were mostly hard packed gravel roads or narrow winding trails. We did every trail that was bike friendly.

Chellberg Farm

The Chellberg Farm was owned and operated by Swedish immigrants, Anders and Johanna Chellberg. It was a working farm for three generations. The house was nice and the turkeys in the coop offered a glimpse of how life may have been in those days.

Hiking

One of my favorite hikes at Indiana Dunes starts at the rear of the Paul H. Douglas Center for Environmental Education. There is a boardwalk that goes by a small pond and then on through a forested area, ending at a dune.

Another great hike at Indiana Dunes State Park is the 3 Dune Challenge. At the end of this hike, you will receive a little award for participation.

Sand Dunes

Sand dunes come in all sizes. This photo is from the top of one sand dune looking down to the beach. Look at the size of the people to get an idea of how high the sand dune is.

House of the Future

The House of the Future competition was part of the 1933 Century of Progress World's Fair in Chicago.

The annual tour is held on the last weekend of September.
The tour is sponsored by the Indiana Landmarks non-profit organization.
Tickets go on sale early in August and usually sell out within one hour.

https://www.indianalandmarks.org

All of these houses are located on Lake Front Drive in the town of Beverly Shores. I really enjoyed seeing these beautiful houses of these futuristic homes. I would have really liked to look inside to see what they perceived as futuristic designs back in that era, but guess I will have to visit in September to see them. I am thinking that it might be similar to the General Electric Carousel of Progress designed by Walt Disney at Disney World, Florida. One thing that I found very interesting is that many of the houses used steel construction.

House of Tomorrow

The house of tomorrow has a first-floor garage and airplane hangar, and for its display at the Worlds Fair, it was photographed with a biplane. Today there are aviation communities around the country with this 'futuristic' design. The use of many windows in this home was way ahead of its time, and proved to be more energy efficient. At the time we visited, it was under a major restoration project.

Florida Tropical House

The majority of Florida homes during the 1930's were of single-story construction and had a smaller footprint, this design would have been somewhat extravagant. This house has an exterior design that would have fit perfectly into Florida housing during that era. Our house in West Hollywood, Florida was stucco with the exterior painted flamingo pink too.

Armco-Ferro House

This is the only remaining house that met all of the competition's design criteria. The construction was simple, utilizing corrugated steel panels that were interchangeable. This design was used after World War II to build homes. This concept may have been the start of prefab homes.

Cypress Log Cabin

I was intrigued by this house because cypress trees are typically found in the south eastern part of the United States. Especially in Florida, houses were made out of cypress trees due to their ability to withstand harsh weather and are bug resistant.

Wieboldt-Rostone House

The Wiebolt-Rostone House is a contemporary structure built using a steel frame clad with Rostone. The original Rostone that was applied to the steel frame did not adhere but another material was applied for refurbishment and was found to be more durable. The arch over the doorway is the original Rostone. This design with the flat roofs remind me more of a Spanish type architecture. When you look at the photo it's hard to believe that it is that old.

12 INDIANA DUNE ACCOMMODATIONS

Camping in the park

Dunewood is the only campground at Indiana Dunes National Park. It is not a large campground. No provided electric or water at the sites. There is, however, a dump station when you leave. See the list of rules, including generator use at: https://www.nps.gov/indu/planyourvisit/permitsandreservations.htm. Sites 1-34 are reservable and sites 35-67 are first come, first serve.

Campground is open April 1 through November 1.

Campground	Phone	Website
Dunewood Campground	877 444-6777	https://www.recreation.gov/

NPS provides a list of maximum vehicle lengths for campsites, and I would use this as a guideline before you try and book a site. One anomaly that I noticed is the way the campground is laid out. Depending what site you select, your door and awning may be opposite of your picnic table location. The campground road is one way and they do not want you to enter in the reverse direction.

Site Dimensions NOTE: ALL VEHICLES MUST BE ON THE DRIVEWAY/PAD

1	Back-in 40 ft, 30x14 pad	2	Back-in 35 ft, 30x14 pad
3	Back-in 46 ft, 28x14 pad	4	Back-in 56 ft, 28x14 pad
5	Back-in 60 ft, 28x14 pad	6	Back-in 40 ft, 28x14 pad
7	Back-in 52 ft, 28x14 pad	8	Back-in 60 ft, 28x14 pad
9	Back-in 46 ft, 30x14 pad	9	Back-in 36 ft, 28x14 pad
10	Back-in 36 ft, 28x14 pad	11	Back-in 40 ft, 30x14 pad
12	Back-in 33 ft, 30x14 pad	13	Back-in 35 ft, 30x14 pad
14	Back-in 48 ft, 28x14 pad	15	Back-in 35 ft, 20x17 pad
16	Back-in 47 ft, 28x14 pad	17	Back-in 39 ft, 28x14 pad
18	Back-in 39 ft, 30x14 pad	19	Back-in 34 ft, 28x14 pad
20	Back-in 44 ft, 28x14 pad	20	Back-in 44 ft, 28x14 pad

21 Back-in 37 ft, 28x14 pad	22	Back-in 46 ft, 28x14 pad
23 Back-in 52 ft, 28x14 pad	24	Back-in 47 ft, 28x14 pad
25 Back-in 48 ft, 28x14 pad	26	Back-in 57 ft, 28x14 pad
27 Back-in 38 ft, 28x14 pad	28	Back-in 47 ft, 28x14 pad
29 Back-in 52 ft, 28x14 pad	30	Back-in 37 ft, 20x17 pad
31 Back-in 50 ft, 28x14 pad	32	Back-in 52 ft, 28x14 pad
33 Back-in 35 ft, 28x14 pad	34	Back-in 33 ft, 28x14 pad

Camping near Indiana Dunes National Park

	Amenities	Phone	Website
Indian Dunes State Park Campground	EL, DS,	219 296-1952	https:// indianastateparks.reservea merica.com/camping/ indiana-dunes/r/ campgroundDetails.do
Sand Creek Campground	EL	219 926-7482	
Michigan City Campground	BR, FH, PT	219 872-7600	https:// michigancitycampground.com
Lakeshore Camp Resort	FH	219 762-7757	http:// lakeshorecampresort.com
Woodland Village RV Lots	BR, FH	219 762-6578	https://wvrvp.com
Sunset Hill Farm County Park Campground	Tents Only	219 465-3586	https:// www.portercountyparks.org/ sunset/camp

Amenities: BR= Big Rigs, WI= Wifi, PO = Pool, FH= Full Hookups, FS= Free NPS Shuttle, DS = Dump Station, PR= Propane, ST= Store, NH= No hookups, SE= Seasonal Rates, DP= Dog Park, SR= Small RV Only, EL= Electric, PT= Pull Through

Hotels near Indiana Dunes

Indiana Dunes is not your typical National Park. It is interwoven with residential areas, a State Park, and large Commercial Properties. Hotels listed below are by town from the National Park Information Center:

Porter - 2 miles south   Chesterton - 2 miles south
Portage - 8 miles southwest   Merrillville - 22 miles southwest
Michigan City - 12 miles northeast

	City	Amenities	Phone	Website
Hilton Garden Inn	Chesterton, IN	FB, FW, FP, PO	219 983-9500	https://www.hilton.com/en/hotels/chictgi-hilton-garden-inn-chesterton/
Quality Inn	Chesterton, IN	FB, FW, FP	219 929-5549	https://www.choicehotels.com/indiana/chesterton/quality-inn-hotels/in389
Best Western Inn & Suites	Chesterton, IN	FB, FW, FP, PO	219 926-2200	https://www.bestwestern.com/en_US/book/hotel-rooms.15095.html
Riley's Railhouse	Chesterton, IN	FB, FW, FP, PF, PO	219 395-9999	https://rileysrailhouse.com
Waterbird Lakeside Inn	Chesterton, IN	FW, FP,	219 928-1501	https://www.waterbirdinn.com
Hampton Inn	Merrillville, IN	FB, FW, FP, PO	219 736-7600	https://www.hilton.com/en/hotels/gyymrhx-hampton-merrillville/
La Quinta Inn	Merrillville, IN	FB, FW, FP, PF, PO	219 738-2870	https://www.wyndhamhotels.com/laquinta/merrillville-indiana/la-quinta-inn-merrillville/overview

	City	Amenities	Phone	Website
Fairfield Inn & Suites	Merrillville, IN	FB, FW, PF	219 736-0500	https://www.marriott.com/hotels/travel/mrvfi-fairfield-inn-and-suites-merrillville/
Residence Inn	Merrillville, IN	FB, FW, FP, PF	219 791-9000	https://www.marriott.com/hotels/travel/mrvri-residence-inn-merrillville/
Home2 Suites	Merrillville, IN	FB, FW, FP, PF, PO	219 769-2620	https://www.hilton.com/en/hotels/gyymeht-home2-suites-merrillville/
Red Roof Inn	Merrillville, IN	FW, FP, PF	219 738-2430	https://www.redroof.com/property/in/merrillville/RRI015
Microtel Inn & Suites	Michigan City, IN	FB, FW, FP, PO	219 210-3430	https://www.wyndhamhotels.com/microtel/michigan-city-indiana/microtel-inn-and-suites-michigan-city/overview
Blue Chip Casino Hotel Spa	Michigan City, IN	PO	219 879-7711	https://www.bluechipcasino.com
Hampton Inn & Suites	Michigan City, IN	FB, FW, FP, PO	219 814-4164	https://www.hilton.com/en/hotels/mgchxhx-hampton-suites-michigan-city/

	City	Amenities	Phone	Website
Baymont by Wyndham	Michigan City, IN	FW, FP, PF, PO	219 210-4384	https://www.wyndhamhotels.com/baymont/michigan-city-indiana/baymont-inn-and-suites-michigan-city/overview
Country Inn and Suites	Michigan City, IN	FB, FW, FP	219 214-4769	https://www.radissonhotels.com/en-us/hotels/country-inn-michigan-city-in
Red Roof Inn	Michigan City, IN	FW, FP, PF	219 874-5251	
Super 8 by Wyndham	Michigan City, IN	FB, FW, FP	219 809-6692	https://www.wyndhamhotels.com/super-8/michigan-city-indiana/super-8-michigan-city/overview
Quality Inn	Michigan City, IN	FB, FW, FP, PO	463 213-2998	https://www.choicehotels.com/indiana/michigan-city/quality-inn-hotels/in415
Hampton Inn	Portage, IN	FB, FW, FP, PF, PO	219 764-1919	https://www.hilton.com/en/hotels/porinhx-hampton-portage/
Super 8 by Wyndham	Portage, IN	FB, FW, FP, PF	219 762-8857	https://www.wyndhamhotels.com/super-8/portage-indiana/super-8-portage/overview
Country Inn and Suites	Portage, IN	FW, FP, PO	219 764-0021	https://www.radissonhotels.com/en-us/hotels/country-inn-portage-in

	City	Amenities	Phone	Website
Days Inn by Wyndham	Portage, IN	FB, FW, FP, PO	219 762-2136	https://www.wyndhamhotels.com/days-inn/portage-indiana/days-inn-portage-in/overview
Baymont by Wyndham	Portage, IN	FB, FW, FP, PF, PO	219 706-3058	https://www.wyndhamhotels.com/baymont/portage-indiana/baymont-portage-indiana-dunes/overview
Best Western Plus	Portage, IN	FB, FW, FP	219 734-6727	https://www.bestwestern.com/en_US/book/hotel-rooms.15104.html
Affordable Suites of America	Portage, IN	FW	219 734-6111	http://www.affordablesuites.com/affordable-suites-portage-in/
Comfort Inn & Suites	Porter, IN	FB, FW, FP	219 250-2181	https://www.choicehotels.com/indiana/porter/comfort-inn-hotels/in253
Spring House Inn	Porter, IN	FB, FW, FP, PO	219 929-4600	https://springhouseinn.com

Amenities: AS= Airport Shuttle /Train Shuttle, FB = Free Breakfast, FCB = Free Continental Breakfast, FW = Free Wifi, FP = Free Parking, PF = Pet Friendly, PO = Pool

13 INDIANA DUNE RESTAURANTS

Restaurants listed below are by town with the distances from the National Park Information Center:

Porter - 2 miles south
Portage - 8 miles southwest
Merrillville - 22 miles southwest
Chesterton - 2 miles south
Michigan City - 12 miles northeast

Note Trip Advisor was current at the time of printing. Please verify again before you make you selection as ratings may change. Rating = rating number 1to 5 and (# of responses).

Types of food Legend

AM = American, BA = Bar, Saloon, Pub or Tavern, BI= Bistro, BK = Bakery, BQ = Barbecue, BR = Breakfast, CA = Cafe, CH = Chinese, CF = Coffee Espresso, CS = Coffee Shop, FF = Fast Food, GR = Grill, HI=Hawaiian, IN = Indian, IT = Italian, JA = Japanese, MD = Mediterranean, MX = Mexican, PZ = Pizza, PO = Polish, SP = Spanish, SE = Seafood, ST = Steakhouse, SU = Sandwich Shop, TH = Thai, UP = Upscale, VE = Vegan

In the table below are restaurants with a Trip Advisor rating of at least four. In the column, 4.5 (233) means a rating of 4.5 (out of 5) with 233 reviews.

Trip Advisor Rating: X.X = # of stars   (XXX) = # of ratings

Porter, Indiana

Name	Trip Advisor	Type	Phone	Website
Country Pride	4.5 (7)	AM	219 926-8566	https://www.ta-petro.com/amenities/restaurants/country-pride
Village Tavern	4 (13)	BA	219 926-5002	https://villagetavern.com

Name	Trip Advisor	Type	Phone	Website
Wagner's Ribs	4.5 (259)	BQ	219 926-7614	https://www.wagnersribs.com
Leroy's "Hot Stuff"	3.5 (33)	MX	219 926-6211	https://leroyshotstuff.business.site
Santiago's Mexican	4 (82)	MX	219 926-6518	https://eatatsantiagos.com

Chesterton, Indiana

Name	Trip Advisor	Type	Phone	Website
Octave Grill	4.5 (308)	AM	219 395-8494	http://www.octavegrill.com
Port Drive In	4 (81)	AM	219 926-3500	https://theportdrivein.net
Round the Clock	4 (81)	AM	219 983-9900	https://www.roundtheclockrestaurants.com
Sunrise Family Restaurant	4 (45)	AM	219 921-1488	https://www.facebook.com/SunriseChesterton/
Craft House	4.5 (108)	BA	219 929-5570	https://www.crafthouse.beer
Gastro 49 Pub & Eatery	4.5 (15)	BA	219 926-1814	https://www.facebook.com/Gastro49/

Name	Trip Advisor	Type	Phone	Website
Third Coast Spice Cafe	4.5 (131)	CA	219 926-5858	https://www.thirdcoastspice.com
Red Cup Cafe & Deli	4 (53)	CA	219 929-1804	https://www.facebook.com/Red-Cup-Cafe-119648684739922/
Tao Chen's	4 (52)	CH	219 926-2542	http://taochenschinese.com
The Original George's Gyros Spot	4 (88)	FF	219 926-5435	https://www.georgesgyrosspot.com
Namaste India	4.5 (34)	IN	219 929-9386	https://www.namasteindiain.com
Lucrezia Cafe	4 (243)	IT	219 926-5829	https://lucreziacafe.com
Villa Nova Pizzeria	4 (45)	IT	219 728-6648	https://www.facebook.com/Villa-Nova-Chesterton-241040262599047/
Musashi	None	JA	219 728-1529	https://musashichesterton.com
Ivy's Bohemia House	4.5 (111)	MD	219 929-4319	https://www.ivysbohemiahouse.com
Lemon Tree Mediterranean Grill	4 (88)	MD	219 926-8733	https://www.lemontreegrill.com

Name	Trip Advisor	Type	Phone	Website
El Cantarito Mexican Cuisine	4 (75)	MX	219 728-6962	https://www.elcantaritocuisine.com
El Salto Mexican	4 (37)	MX	219 395-9890	https://www.elsaltorestaurant.com
Ajs Pizza	4.5 (80)	PZ	219 464-8282	https://ajspizzaco.com
Gelsosomo's Pizzeria	4 (120)	PZ	219 926-6363	http://www.gelpizza.com
Duneland Pizza	4.5 (48)	PZ	219 926-1163	http://www.dunelandpizza.com
Val's Famous Pizza & Grinders	4 (76)	PZ	219 921-0056	http://www.valsfamouspizzaandgrinders.com
Brown Bag Sandwich Shop	5 (10)	SU	219 787-8193	https://zmenu.com/brown-bag-sandwich-shop-chesterton-online-menu/

Portage, Indiana

Name	Trip Advisor	Type	Phone	Website
Tate's Place	4.5 (123)	AM	219 764-8283	https://tatesplace.food87.com
House of Pancakes	4.5 (101)	AM	219 762-9588	https://www.zmenu.com/portage-house-of-pancakes-portage-online-menu/

Name	Trip Advisor	Type	Phone	Website
Schoop's Hamburgers	4 (56)	AM	219 763-1410	https://www.schoophamburgers.com
Rosewood Family Restaurant	4 (34)	AM	219 763-3297	https://rosewoodfamilyrestaurants.com
First Wok	4 (10)	CH	219 762-8858	http://www.firstwokportage.com
Depot Hot Dogs	4.5 (37)	FF	219 406-0900	https://indulgery.com/b/depot-hot-dogs-portage
Fuji Japanese	4.5 (50)	JA	219 763-4131	https://www.facebook.com/fujijapanese/
JC's Bocatas	Facebook 4.5 (54)	MX	219 841-9523	https://www.jcbocatas.com
El Pueblo	4 (26)	MX	219 764-8226	https://www.facebook.com/ElPuebloMexicanRestaurant
El Amigo	4 (12)	MX	219 763-3833	https://www.facebook.com/El-Amigo-3-1484075658535238/
La Cabana	4 (11)	MX	219 254-2078	https://lacabanarestaurants.com
Cappos	4 (107)	PZ	219 762-5563	https://www.capposcasualdining.com

Name	Trip Advisor	Type	Phone	Website
Gelsosomo's Pizzeria	4 (65)	PZ	219 763-1545	http://www.gelpizza.com
BAM Pizza Company	4.5 (33)	PZ	219 763-1767	https://www.bampizzaco.com
Longhorn Steakhouse	4 (168)	ST	219 762-5911	https://www.longhornsteakhouse.com/locations/in/portage/portage/5279
Texas Roadhouse	4 (83)	ST	219 762-5900	https://www.texasroadhouse.com/locations/indiana/portage

Michigan City, Indiana

Name	Trip Advisor	Type	Phone	Website
Holly's	4.5 (770)	AM	219 879-5124	http://www.hollysrestaurant.com
Bridges Waterside Grille	4 (241)	AM	219 878-0227	http://bridgeswatersidegrille.com
Fiddleheads	4 (200)	AM	219 210-3253	https://fiddleheadmc.com
Hammer's Food & Drink	4.5 (65)	AM	219 879-0760	http://www.hammersrestaurant.com

Name	Trip Advisor	Type	Phone	Website
McGinnis Pub	4 (117)	BA	219 872-8200	http://mcginnispub.com/index.html
The Game	4 (86)	BA	219 879-7711	https://www.bluechipcasino.com/dine/the-game
Taverna Tonelli	4 (79)	BA	219 221-6453	https://www.tavernatonelli.com/menu
Swingbelly's	4 (59)	BA	219 874-5718	https://swingbellys.org
Sophia's House of Pancakes	4.5 (260)	BR	219 879-9999	http://www.sophiasmichigancity.com
Memo's House of Pancakes	4 (52)	BR	219 871-1583	https://www.memoshousofpancakes.com
Dune Billies Beach Cafe	4.5 (42)	CA	219 809-6592	https://dunebilliesbeachcafe.com
Cool Runnings	Facebook 5 (307)	CC	219 210-3885	https://www.facebook.com/CoolRunningsIN/
Schoop's Hamburgers	4.5 (133)	FF	219 872-0170	https://www.schoophamburgers.com
Carlson's Drive-In	4.5 (114)	FF	219 872-0331	https://www.carlsonsdrivein.com

Name	Trip Advisor	Type	Phone	Website
India House	4 (61)	IN	219 874-5700	http://www.indiahousein.site
Olive Garden	4 (59)	IT	219 879-6830	https://www.olivegarden.com/locations/in/michigan-city/michigan-city-franklin-street/1810
Hokkaido Japanese	4.5 (48)	JA	219 814-4226	https://www.facebook.com/sushimichigancity/
Sake Asian Fusion	Facebook 5 (37)	JA	219 809-0111	https://sakeasianfusionin.com
Mucho Mas	4.5 (80)	MX	219 221-6639	https://www.facebook.com/MuchoMC/
El Cajete	4.5 (70)	MX	219 872-3333	http://www.elcajeterestaurant.com
El Bracero	4 (70)	MX	219 872-0760	https://www.facebook.com/El-Bracero-of-Michigan-City-Indiana-113411668692483/
Polish Peasant	5 (57)	PO	219 873-1788	https://www.facebook.com/The-Polish-Peasant-114705872511030/
Albano's Villa	4 (105)	PZ	219 872-0571	http://albanosvilla.com
Gelsosomo's Pizzeria	4 (47)	PZ	219 872-3838	http://www.gelpizza.com

Name	Trip Advisor	Type	Phone	Website
Bartlett's Fish Camp	4 (123)	SE	219 879-9544	https://bartlettsfishcamp.hrpos.heartland.us/menu
Red Lobster	4 (78)	SE	219 879-1328	https://www.redlobster.com/locations/list/in/michigan-city/4353-franklin-street
Galveston Steakhouse	4.5 (286)	ST	219 879-5555	https://www.facebook.com/Galveston-Steakhouse-221151807834/
Pactrick's Grille	4.5 (66)	ST	219 873-9401	http://www.patricksgrille.com
Panini Panini	5 (364)	SU	219 873-1720	https://www.paninipaniniin.com/?utm_source=bing&utm_medium=websiteurl&utm_campaign=search#/

Merrillville, Indiana

Name	Trip Advisor	Type	Phone	Website
Cooper's Hawk Winery & Restaurant	4.5 (298)	AM	219 795-9463	https://chwinery.com
Cracker Barrel	4 (130)	AM	219 947-2617	https://locations.crackerbarrel.com/in/merrillville/84/
Cafe Fondue	4.5 (61)	AM	219 793-1511	http://www.cafefondue.net

Name	Trip Advisor	Type	Phone	Website
Round the Clock	4 (35)	AM	219 769-1591	https://roundtheclock.com
Bar Louie	4 (66)	BA	219 793-9340	https://www.barlouie.com/locations/us/in/merrillville/merrillville
Brothers Breakfast	5 (8)	BR	219 769-1591	https://www.dineatbrothers.com
Grand Park Cafe	4.5 (16)	CA	219 769-1234	https://www.facebook.com/Grand-park-cafe-770794849974278/
Portillo's Hot Dogs	4.5 (544)	FF	219 769-8300	https://www.portillos.com/locations/merrillville/?utm_source=listings&utm_medium=yext&utm_campaign=website
Chili's Grill	4 (37)	GR	219 791-1504	https://www.chilis.com/locations/us/IN/Hobart/
Taste of India	4 (68)	IN	219 755-4634	https://www.merrillvilletasteofindia.com
Gamba Ristorante	4.5 (134)	IT	219 736-5000	https://www.gambaristorante.com
Olive Garden	3.5 (109)	IT	219 769-2479	https://www.olivegarden.com/locations/in/merrillville/merrillville-westfield-south-lake-mall/1106
House of Kobe	4 (118)	JA	219 791-9500	https://houseofkobe.com

Name	Trip Advisor	Type	Phone	Website
Aladdin Pita	4.5 (74)	MD	219 736-5204	https://www.aladdinpita.com
Villa Del Sol Mexican	4 (33)	MX	219 750-9137	https://www.facebook.com/VillaDelSolInMerrillville/
El Salto Mexican	4 (24)	MX	219 940-9955	https://www.elsaltorestaurant.com
El Chaparral Mexican	4.5 (15)	MX	219 472-0328	https://www.elchaparralmexicanrestaurant.com
Old Chicago	4 (171	PZ	219 472-0616	https://oldchicago.com/locations/merrillville
Maxim's	4 (43)	PZ	219 472-6603	https://www.maximsrestaurant.com
Red Lobster	4 (84)	SE	219 769-0500	https://www.redlobster.com/locations/list/in/merrillville/1450-e-82nd-ave
Gino's Steakhouse	4 (214)	ST	219 769-4466	https://sites.google.com/site/ginossteakhouse/
Texas Corral	4 (22)	ST	219 769-1101	https://texascorral.net
Panera Bread	4 (49)	SU	219 756-3550	https://locations.panerabread.com/in/merrillville/303-east-81st-avenue.html

Name	Trip Advisor	Type	Phone	Website
Potbelly Sandwich Shop	4 (23)	SU	219 736-9616	https://www.potbelly.com/stores/23142
Asparagus	4.5 (247)	TH	219 794-0000	https://asparagusrestaurant.com
Spice Thai Cuisine	4.5 (23)	TH	219 769-7696	http://www.spicethaicuisinemerrillville.com
Saigon Noodle House	4.5 (12)	VI	219 769-8508	https://www.zmenu.com/saigon-noodle-house-merrillville-online-menu/

14 INDIANA DUNE TRANSPORTATION

AMTRAK Train Information

The closest public transportation for both airline and rail travel will be through Chicago, IL.

Chicago, IL Amtrak

Several Amtrak lines connect through Union Station in Chicago, IL. The lines include:

Blue Water, Cardinal, Capitol Limited, Empire Builder, Illinois Zephyr, Lincoln Service, and Pere Marquette

Amtrak Website: https://www.amtrak.com/home

Airline Information

There are two airports that service the Chicago metro area. O'Hare International Airport is significantly larger than Midway International Airport, and both are convenient to Indiana Dunes National Park.

Chicago, IL, O'Hare International Airport (ORD) - Chicago, IL
https://www.flychicago.com/ohare/home/pages/default.aspx

Company	Phone	Website
Aer Lingus	800-474-7424	http://www.aerlingus.com/
AeroMexico	800-237-6639	http://www.aeromexico.com/
Air Canada	888-247-2262	http://www.aircanada.com/
Air Choice One	866-435-9847	http://www.airchoiceone.com/

Company	Phone	Website
Air France	800-237-2747	http://www.airfrance.com/indexCOM.html
Air India	800-621-8231	http://www.airindia.com/
Air New Zealand	800-262-1234	https://www.airnewzealand.com/
Alaska Airlines	800-252-7522	https://www.alaskaair.com/
Alitalia	800-223-5730	https://www.alitalia.com/en_us/
All Nippon ANA	800-235-9262	http://www.ana.co.jp/asw/wws/us/e/
American Airlines	800 433-7300	http://www.aa.com
Austrian Airlines	800-843-0002	http://www.austrian.com/en_us/
Boutique Air	855-268-8478	http://www.BoutiqueAir.com
British Airways	800-247-9297	http://www.britishairways.com/travel/home/public/en_us
Cape Air	800-227-3247	https://www.capeair.com/where_we_fly/Midwest/midwest.html
Cathay Pacific Airways	800-233-2742	http://www.cathaypacific.com/cx/en_US.html
China Eastern Airlines	800-321-8900	http://us.ceair.com/en/
Copa Airlines	800-359-2672	https://www.copaair.com/en/web/us
Delta	800 221-1212	http://www.delta.com/

Company	Phone	Website
EVA Air	847-261-9900	https://www.evaair.com/en-us/index.html
Emirates	888-320-1576	https://www.emirates.com/
Ethiopian Airlines	800-445-2733	http://www.ethiopianairlines.com/
Etihad Airways	877-690-0767	http://flights.etihad.com/en-us/
Finnair	877-757-7143	https://www.finnair.com/us/gb/
Frontier	801 401-9000	http://www.flyfrontier.com
Hainan Airlines	888-688-8813	https://www.hainanairlines.com/CN/GB/Welcome
Iberia Airlines	800-772-4642	http://www.iberia.com/
Icelandair	800-223-5500	http://www.icelandair.us/
Interjet Airlines	866-285-9525	http://www.interjet.com/en-us
Japan Airlines (JAL)	800-525-3663	http://www.jal.co.jp/en/
JetBlue	800-538-2583	http://www.jetblue.com/#/
KLM Royal Dutch	800-618-0104	http://www.klm.com/
Korean Air	800-438-5000	https://www.koreanair.com/global/en.html
LOT Polish Airlines	212-789-0970	http://www.lot.com/pl/pl/

Company	Phone	Website
Lufthansa	800-645-3880	http://www.lufthansa.com/online/portal/lh/us/homepage
Norwegian	800-357-4159	https://www.norwegian.com/us/
Qatar Airways	877-777-2827	http://www.qatarairways.com/us/en/homepage.page
Royal Jordanian	212-949-0050	http://www.rj.com/en
Swiss	877-359-7947	https://www.swiss.com/us/en
Scandinavian Airlines (SAS)	800-221-2350	http://www.flysas.com/
Spirit Airlines	855-728-3555	https://www.spirit.com/
Sun Country Airlines	651-905-2737	https://www.suncountry.com/booking/search.html
TAP Air Portugal	800-221-7370	https://www.flytap.com/en-us/
Turkish Airlines	800-874-8875	http://www.turkishairlines.com/
United	800-864-8331	https://www.united.com/ual/en/us/?root=1
VivaAerobus	888-935-9848	https://www.vivaaerobus.com/en
Volaris Airlines	866-988-3527	http://volaris.com/

Chicago, IL O'Hare International Airport Car Rental

Company	Phone	Website
Alamo	844 354-6962	avis.com

Company	Phone	Website
Avis	773 825-4600	enterprise.com
Budget	800 218-7992	budget.com
Dollar	800 800-4000	dollar.com
Enterprise	855 266-9289	enterprise.com
Fox	323 593-7485	foxrentacar.com
Hertz	800 654-3131	hertz.com
National	800 367-6767	nationalcar.com
Payless	800 729-5377	paylesscar.com
Routes Car Rental	800 467-6883	routes.ca
Sixt	888 749-8227	sixt.com
Thrifty	800 847-4389	thrifty.com

Chicago, IL, Midway International Airport (MDW) - Chicago, IL
https://www.flychicago.com/midway/home/pages/default.aspx

Company	Phone	Website
Allegiant	702 505-8888	https://www.allegiantair.com
Delta	800 221-1212	delta.com
Porter Airlines	888-619-8622	http://www.flyporter.com/
Southwest Airlines	800-435-9792	http://www.southwest.com/
Volaris Airlines	866-988-3527	http://volaris.com/

Chicago, IL Midway International Airport Car Rental

Company	Phone	Website
Alamo	800 327-9633	alamo.com
Avis	800 331-1212	avis.com
Budget	800 527-7000	budget.com
Dollar	800 800-4000	dollar.com
Enterprise	800 566-9249	enterprise.com
Hertz	800 654-3131	hertz.com
National	800 227-7368	nationalcar.com
Thrifty	800 527-7075	thrifty.com

15 PARK UNITS NEAR INDIANA DUNES

Distance chart from Indiana Dunes and Gateway Arch

Park Unit	City/State	Indiana Dunes NP Driving Time	Distance
Lincoln Home National Historic Site	Springfield, IL	3h 15m	220 miles
Pullman National Monument	Chicago, IL	37m	38 miles
George Rogers Clark National Historic Site	Vincennes, IN	3h 56m	234 miles
Lincoln Boyhood National Memorial	Lincoln City, IN	4h 48m	297 miles
Lewis & Clark National Historic Trail	IA, ID, IL, IN, KS, KY, MO, MT, NE, ND, OH, OR, PA, SD, WA, WV	N/A	N/A
Mormon Pioneer National Historic Trail	IL, IA, NE, UT, WY	N/A	N/A
Trail of Tears National Historic Trail	AL, AR, GA, IL, KY, MO, NC, OK, TN	N/A	N/A

Lincoln Home National Historic Site

Address: 413 S. 8th Street, Springfield, IL, 62701
Phone: 217 492-4241
Website: https://www.nps.gov/liho/index.htm

Overview: Lincoln Home National Historic Site was established in 1971 and has about 12.2 acres.
The Lincoln's lived here between 1844 and 1861 and this location is in a residential area and parking may be a challenge. The site does have a small pay-for-parking lot adjacent the Visitor Center. During your visit, view the feature film and take a ranger-led tour of Lincoln's home. Take a walk around the neighborhood and see the Jameson Jenkins lot (site of the Underground Railroad), Rosenwald House (former president of Sears, Roebuck & Company), and twelve other historic sites.

Pullman National Monument

Address: 11141 S. Cottage Grove, Chicago, IL, 60628
Phone: 773 768-9310
Website: https://www.nps.gov/pull/index.htm

Overview: Pullman Historic District was added to the National Register of Historic Places in 1969 and became a US National Historic Landmark in 1970, a Chicago Landmark in 1972, and finally a National Monument in 2015. Pullman National Monument encompasses 230 acres.

George Mortimer Pullman purchased 4,000 acres in Chicago to establish a factory and a community for the workers that would build Pullman Railroad Cars. This community provided housing for its factory workers, which was somewhat of a new concept, with a peak of 8,000 workers. His idea of a model town latter proved to be a bad investment.

Pullman National Monument has a great Visitor Information Center and museum. You can take a map for a self-guided tour or schedule a ranger-led tour by calling: 773 768-9310.

George Rogers Clark National Historic Site

Address: 401 S. 2nd Street, Vincennes, IN 47591
Phone: (812) 882-1776 x1210
Website: https://www.nps.gov/gero/index.htm

Overview: In 1779, Colonel George Rogers Clark marched in the bitter cold and freezing waters to Fort Sackville, where the British surrendered without a shot being fired. This accomplishment expanded the northern frontier and was almost as large as the original 13 colonies.

George Rogers Clark was the older brother to William Clark of the Lewis and Clark Corps of Discovery. It was George Rogers Clark that President Thomas Jefferson initially wanted to lead the expedition, however, it was delayed until after the Louisiana Purchase took place with the French in 1803. Meriwether Lewis was selected by President Jefferson to the lead the expedition and he offered a position to William Clark, George Rogers Clark's younger brother, to share the command on the expedition.

The monument and his bronze statue are only open from 9 am to 4:45 pm, 7 days a week.

Lincoln Boyhood National Memorial

Address: 3027 East South Street, Lincoln City, IN 47552
Phone: 812 937-4541
Website: https://www.nps.gov/libo/index.htm

Overview: The Visitor Center provides exhibits, video, and gift shop. The grounds are open from sunrise to sunset and the Visitor Center is open 9 am to 5 pm daily.

As a child, Abraham Lincoln had many influences in his life. His father, Thomas Lincoln, had the same traits (honest, God fearing, respectful, and a storyteller) that we think of when we reflect on Abraham Lincoln, the man. His mother, Nancy Hanks Lincoln, even though not educated, sought for her son to be educated. After Nancy's death, Abraham's stepmother, Sarah Bush Johnston Lincoln, continued his education.

Take a short hike to visit the grave of Nancy Hanks Lincoln, and see the small foundation of the cabin that he grew up in as a boy. This a pet friendly hiking area.

Lewis & Clark National Historic Trail
IA, ID, IL, IN, KS, KY, MO, MT, NE, ND, OH, OR, PA, SD, WA,WV

Address: 601 Riverfront Drive, Omaha, NE, 68102
Phone: 402 661-1804
Website: https://www.nps.gov/lecl/index.htm

The Lewis and Clark National Historic Trail is approximately 4,900 miles long, extending from Pittsburgh, Pennsylvania, to the mouth of the Columbia River, near present day Astoria, Oregon. It follows the historic outbound and inbound routes of the Lewis and Clark Expedition as well as the preparatory section from Pittsburgh, Pennsylvania to Wood River, Illinois.
Source: NPS

Mormon Pioneer National Historic Trail
IL, IA, NE UT, WY

Address: PO Box 728, Santa Fe, MM, 87504
Phone: 505 988-6098
Website: https://www.nps.gov/mopi/index.htm

Overview: Explore the Mormon Pioneer National Historic Trail across five states to see the 1,300-mile route traveled by Mormons who fled Nauvoo, Illinois, to the Great Salt Lake Valley in 1846-1847.
Source: NPS

Trail Of Tears National Historic Trail
AL, AR, GA, IL, KY, MO, NC, OK, TN

Address: PO Box 728, Santa Fe, MM, 87504
Phone: 505 988-6098
Website: https://www.nps.gov/trte/index.htm

Remember and commemorate the survival of the Cherokee people, forcefully removed from their homelands in Georgia, Alabama, and Tennessee to live in Indian Territory, now Oklahoma. They traveled by foot, horse, wagon, or steamboat in 1838-1839.
Source: NPS

16 NATIONAL PARK PLANNING GUIDES

Other National Park Planning Guides are available on my Amazon author page at: https://www.amazon.com/Kenneth-Perry/e/B06XTZFYN8?ref=sr_ntt_srch_lnk_1&qid=1630800482&sr=8-1.

Title	States	Edition	Paperback ISBN	eBook ISBN
Badlands and Wind Cave National Parks Planning Guide	SD	2nd	978-1-94649 0-14-8	978-1-946490-13-1
Carlsbad Caverns and Guadalupe National Parks Planning Guide	NM, TX	2nd	978-1-94649 0-20-9	978-1-946490-22-3
Dry Tortugas and Biscayne National Parks Planning Guide	FL	2nd	978-1-94649 0-16-2	978-1-946490-15-5
Gateway Arch and Indiana Dunes National Parks Planning Guide	MO, IN	1st	978-1-94649 0-39-1	978-1-946490-38-4
Glacier National Park Planning Guide	MT	2nd	978-1-94649 0-34-6	978-1-946490-21-6
Grand Canyon National Park Planning Guide	AZ	1st	978-1-94649 0-30-8	978-1-946490-29-2
Grand Canyon and Petrified Forest National Parks Planning Guide	AZ	1st	978-1-94649 0-24-7	978-1-946490-23-0
Hawaiian Islands National Park Planning Guide	HI	1st	978-1-94649 0-41-4	978-1-946490-40-7

Title	States	Edition	Paperback ISBN	eBook ISBN
Joshua Tree National Park Planning Guide	CA	1st	978-1-94649 0-26-1	978-1-946490-25-4
Petrified Forest National Park Planning Guide	AZ	1st	978-1-94649 0-32-2	978-1-946490-31-5
Redwood National Park Planning Guide	CA	1st	978-1-94649 0-28-5	978-1-946490-27-8
Theodore Roosevelt National Park Planning Guide	ND	1st	978-1-94649 0-37-7	978-1-946490-36-0
Yellowstone National Park Planning Guide	WY, MT, ID	1st	978-1-94649 0-12-4	978-1-946490-11-7
Zion & Bryce Canyon National Parks Planning Guide	UT	2nd	978-1-94649 0-18-6	978-1-946490-17-9

17 ABOUT THE AUTHOR

Kenneth Perry has visited all 50 of the United States. In addition, he has also visited many European countries, the Caribbean, Mexico, and Canada. As Ken got closer to retirement age, he had a revelation; he had done a lot of traveling, but he had never really explored all the natural beauty and resources here in the United States.

One of Ken's bucket list items was to visit all of the National Parks and National Monuments with his wife, Cindy. Ken has visited 38 National Parks and 33 National Monuments and many of the other NPS units. As of April 2021, there are 61 National Parks and 88 National Monuments. Ken and Cindy will be traveling in their motor home to visit most of the parks, excluding Hawaii and the Virgin Islands. Bailey, their dog, has also been quite the little traveler.

With an engineering and management background and extensively planning family vacations and camp outs, Ken decided to use his experience in the development of planning guides.

Ken is a Certified Interpretive Guide and has provided interpretive "Red Bus" tours at Glacier National Park, Yellow Bus and the large bus tours at Yellowstone, and an Interpretive Park Ranger at Fort Union Trading Post National Historic Site.

Have a great adventure!
Kenneth Perry

ISBN-10: - 1-946490-39-3
ISBN-13: - 978-1-946490-39-1